Loud

To Andy
Now that I have Signed this, you cannot sell this on amazon and other online stores.

David Davies

Ha Ha ha ha ha haaaaaa

All the Best
David.

Buzz Records UK

30 Princess Elzellia Court

Nature-vale manor BT8 8GB

Northern Ireland

Printed by www.createspace.com

For indie publishing BuzzRecords UK ©

Published by BuzzRecords © 01/09/2018

Contents

"In the 1930s, both Sartre and Merleau-Ponty saw phenomenology as a means of going beyond narrow empiricist, psychological assumptions about human existence, broadening the scope of philosophy to be about everything, to capture life as it is lived."

Moran, Dermot

"...a man wants to live in a shell. He wants the walls that protect him to be as smoothly polished and as firm as if his sensitive flesh had to come in direct contact with them. The shell confers a daydream of purely physical intimacy."

Gaston, Bachelard

Dearly Remembered
Ninda
Gwyneth Davies

Into the Wild

(An introduction influenced by the Song 'Lonesome Dreams' By Lord Huron.)

It is beautiful to see the Crested Grebes in their courtship dance during spring, as they mimic each other's body language in perfect harmony. The murmuration of Starlings has this ability to connect with each other in flight, so that they do not pump into each other as they change direction in synchronicity, giving them the ability to create beautiful shapes that carve into the evening sky. We too mimic each other, especially when we like or fancy a person. The gestures is also done in synchronicity like the folding of arms and putting hands up to rest on the chin, as if a duet. Even the sounding of laughs and words can seem impersonated. I feel you can also touch or comfort someone through electrical invisible charges that tickles the heart, in other words kinetic energy. Even when someone dies in the family their body language, facially expressions and attitudes can still live on in us. That's why it is important to endure the pain of loss, for the sake of love. I only met my Dad briefly when I was a baby, he died when I was just three months old. My Mum always notices that I do some things that my Dad had done, certain habits and mannerisms. These are the memories and their spirit that lives in the subconscious. I believe the subconscious is a form that connects us all, which creates this mimicking bound that we see in marriage and in couples. Or perhaps if you have done something wrong, the guilty conscience can be a hindrance and a betrayal for us. The embarrassed flushes of perhaps what you have done in the spare quiet moments in seclusion, or revealing that you fancy someone, and she stands before you, your eyes turn shyly to the ground. Therefor we must be connected and communicate on a spiritually conscious or subconscious level like telepathy. Though it can become a mental warfare with intruding voices and thoughts that can bully, deceive and threaten us, creating fear. The child within us or the good voice is too often suppressed and cut out from being heard by noise. This belief is surrounded by my own experience of how noise has hurt me mentally and in the consequence has given me understanding to my self-contained consciousness. It is the start to social isolation and with less interaction from the public in our day to day lives, living with mental illness is very lonely. Even as simple as a hello, can help us feel to belong, to be part of something. The poem titled 'Mr Kiss finds himself in a House Party' is about social isolation where we can experience loneliness in a public place, feeling detached from those around us, and how one might feel within? Creating supressed emotions.

I believe noise affects us all, on a day to day basis, provoking and annoying us. We may not be aware of sounds that lurk, hum, buzz and thud in the background from car alarms, repetitious beeps and other various machines and mod-coms; but it is there and I feel creates more stress for all of us. Noise is even benefited in training dogs by a clicking device that is used when the dog miss-behaves, the dog quickly remembers by the pain so often afflicted on him. Likewise, at a certain level, a bouncing noise can act as a deterrent for mice, you just plug the device into the wall. So noise must affect us human beings at certain levels giving us less concentration, disrupting our sleep patterns and blocking our connection with others.

Moreover to the above, our subconscious can also be connected to objects leaving a voice or memory to be felt and heard. Though sadly I believe this can also be disturbed and suppressed through noise. This is 'containment', separated from objects and people around us. Objects can leave such a power of sentiment value that a hoarder will feel they are throwing out a part of a person, a piece of themselves or a memory, consequently they will keep and treasure every object. This is the desire to experience romanticism in our stressful modern world and to hold on to others i.e. loved ones and those we miss; to hold on to the comfort of a memory.

I am writing about this to illustrate the despair and repression that I have went through, all because of noise. It has caused my life to be miserable, where my anxiety disorder has manifested itself in aches and pains throughout my body. I also experience my legs and arms twitching uncontrollably as I rest or try and go to sleep, this is the mental scaring due to constant disturbance of sleep. Unnecessary random noise is intrusive and invasive that has hurt my mind and stomach, which I feel has contributed to the cause of disorders such as IBS, impotence and anxiety disorder. Impotence is a very embarrassing subject for males; but being a sufferer I wanted to let others know that they are not alone. The function of my penis works randomly, sometimes I cannot ejaculate even from the hardest effort, and my erection could cut out during sex, and at worst cannot even get an erection. A man's apparatus is his confidence, and when it stops working it is a big issue. I felt useless, the whole point of life, is the hope for a life; to help bring into the world a child. The contact and affection part of sex is important too, it is an act to participate and to appreciate each other when in love.

The poem in this collection titled 'Symptoms of Suppression' is a study about my panic attacks caused by noise, it also illustrates these conditions as (above). Thus creating my mind to change unpredictably to moods such as aggression and panic.

Translating and expressing feelings to the outside world is hard for a child, it is now that I am older that I can attempt to express my inner child. Behavioural problems can usually be a result of emotions that are trapped, wanting to say something to the outside world and wanting to be heard. But these feelings build up inside to explode into outbursts, anger, and frustration, self-harm and suicide attempts, which are usually a cry for help. The question is, am I a product of society? What I mean is, is my mental illness caused by the things around and imposed upon me, such as noise? Wrapped and contained until my packaging bursts and it seems nobody wants damaged goods. Though the subject of intrusive voices and thoughts is vast and needs further writing, my main aim and concern is to express a protest against my sensitivity to noise. I feel that noise is attacking me, which it has supressed my emotions, conscience and connection to others, thus leading to behavioural problems. The pain that noise causes my mind and body is also another reason to cry for help.

The Devil's Shelf

What packaging is around the contents?
Is it what you want to see or read?
Bright logo, printed to represent an image;
But what is the ingredients? So easily missed

What calories does it hold?
Could it be used to rote teeth?
Is it set with a good expensive make?
Made naturally, organically
As if a natural birth,

Packed and surrounded by plastic
If damaged, is there any worth?
Low on the bottom shelf
Many pass…
And even if a child brings to attention
(Being at their eye level) this odd product,
It is however, a knocked over bag that is leaking
With a trail of white sugar.
Surely that is, it's weak packaging speaking.

Then brings to sight an old sticky sweet
Covered in dirt, dust and other bits,
Just lying on the supermarket floor.

I do not call 'sound' noise, as the word 'noise' seems to possess a harshness; but 'sound' carries a softer presence. For example you would not say "The noise of the birds singing is charming." But rather "The sound of the birds singing is charming."

Our temporal domain of technology possesses this 'noise' that causes stress. For me it is a case of technology vs nature with so much of our inventions harming us and nature. Though noise and sound can collaborate to express these stresses and their battle by organising these elements in music. The piece is then arranged in a way to create rhythm, or perhaps not, maybe to have rhythm interrupted by harsh unorganised noise. Artists such as 'future sound of London' and 'Nine Inch Nails' do a good study of industrial sound mixed with rhythm, music and on occasions the beauty. Many noises lurk in the peaceful summer night air, a high pitch sound intrudes through my opened window, you can barely notice it, if it was not for my sensitivity to noise, as I lay in bed looking up to the stars.

*

Music for me is a powerful medium and has spoken to me in many levels of emotions that has helped me to identify with love, pain and heartache; death, religion and mental illness etc. These questions are so often asked and thrown around to form ideas and beliefs. There has been so many writers, musicians and painters that have influenced the way I think. It helps me to reason with my personal life and what causes us to retreat so much in a society that is called social? Where more times than often these musicians have expressed their pain and hurt in our society. It is this empathy that we have with them, having similar feelings like loneliness making the songs more potent to the listener. Music has the ability to captivate my heart, it is, and I feel that words are at their most powerful, when they are carried by music.

The song that I have used for an example is 'Lonesome Dreams' by Lord Huron. The words convey a man, an adventurer, perhaps shipwrecked:

"I land on an island coast
Where the only souls I see are ghosts"

This makes me think of the quote by John Donne *"no man is an island."* An island is to be self-sufficient, producing what is available from the islands resources, perhaps to be self-willed and proud; but I feel that this island is not an option, as we are isolated due to various issues such as mental illness and loneliness, thus being forced to be on our own island. I agree with John Donne's statement giving that we all need help, though sometimes our dreams is a place that we need to retreat to, like a far distant shore and music is a tool to help us engage with our imagination, giving us unlimited possibilities.

When being lost (mentally ill), I feel people become more desirable, yet more unattainable *"... search all day, never find anyone."* It is like a child dreaming of her prince, the built in dreams from childhood influence of stories, which is similar to the girl in the film 'Labyrinth' where she is tempted with the safety of her bedroom, with her dreams of being a princess; but outside the bedroom is reality of some apocalyptic landscape. Though in the film the outside is a junk yard landscape that stretches for miles; to compare, our world is as equally a place of hostility, where we need our safe haven to dream like a beautiful distant island. The juxtaposing of interior and exterior, the private and the public, the physical space and mental space. These worlds can collide or cause friction on each other, this being that inside could be lonely without the attachment to people, causing the interior to be fooled as if inside is safer, thus causing you to miss out on friendship and the outside world, in other words we should push oneself out of our comfort zone.

"If there is one enemy of romanticism, it is containment: the acceptance of imposed limits and external order, of irredeemable separateness of objects and people, emotions and ideas, the divine and the earthly, or, as Mariele Neudecker put it in one of her titles, Heaven, the sky."

Eszter Barbarczy

"I have been dreaming again of a lonesome world." Sometimes through pain and isolation we can fall in love with loneliness, it could be similar to the 'Stockholm syndrome' where constant isolation (in this case, mental illness and fear is the kidnapper) can make us happy and dependant with the situation. Frightened to go out, and a longing to be away from the busy, fast paced flow of life, where there are millions of people just over the doorstep.

It is brave to take a step into the pulsing complexity of the city's landscape with the expanse of the sky seldom seen, just hints of blue teasing us of freedom. Idle buildings that grow grey and tall in their closeness and grotesque forms, what square gives a choice, edged with hard points? The corners of the modern buildings so prudent and staunch in their strict precise lines. In early Sunday evening during winter, the shops close with a wet, damp and cold rain. Looking up to see the lights go out then the ghostly shadows appear in empty work buildings. The shady out of sight worlds glanced through dark windows; the thought of what could lurk and move within creates a chill inside. These worlds stretch from city to city, and of course travelling around the world is adventurous; but on your own everyone seems the same, and there is always a girl in your heart back home that you cannot let go. In every face I see her, every turn and twist, where my mind is engulfed by such beautiful loneliness. Maybe Lord Huron uses the word 'Ghosts' as a metaphor that represents past relationships, which have maybe failed or regrets of past opportunities.

"Who has not deep in his heart
A dark castle of Elsinore

In the manner of men of the past
We build within ourselves stone
On stone a vast haunted castle."

Vincent Monteiro

The song 'Lonesome Dreams' has influenced me with many ideas, perhaps my first floor flat is a wooden shelter upon a small 'knoll' looking across, where my mind is the wild landscape as vast as the planet. I gaze through my window of what could lurk outside, the possibility of many creeping animals, maybe a roaring tiger under a crystal clear sky, pinned with stars of earnest creativity, a werewolf's full moon of an inner monster. This is the window of expression taking me out of myself and into a world of writing.

"A lighthouse catches sight
Or to chase away what may fright
Like snow upon a woodland floor
Carpets its torch
Illuminating corners,
To ease away this night."

I also feel the song urging me to be out walking amidst nature as an adventurer without people and technology. This reminisces on the film 'into the wild', where a young adult undertakes a journey and adventures into the Alaskan wilderness to be with nature, to be free and self-sufficient. It is like a call to try and go back to Eden, to a place of beauty and contentment, and the earth is as fresh as when it was first made. The ghosts mentioned in the song could indicate that mankind has left their mark in every corner of the world, a sad state for the explorers, and when Lord Huron uses the words "I have been dreaming again of a lonesome world." You can't help but think that they mean an untouched world. 'Into the wild' – such a landscape usually offers peace, freedom and contentment; but the parody is we need people; but they are amongst city dwellings, where so much can conflict our minds. Mental illness causes us to struggle, not being able to adapt within these modern environments, causing us to retreat or become recluse.

In the times of the great ancient dynasties some people lived recluse in the middle of a great wilderness; but for them it was a choice, and the landscape was a long love affair.

"Nothing like all the others, even as a child,
Rooted in such love for hills and mountains,

I stumble into their net of dust, that one
Departure a blunder lasting thirteen years."
T'ao Ch'ien (365 – 427 AD)

Lord Huron sings during the verse *"But I don't really know this place, and its lonesome here in a wide open space"*, perhaps realising when it is too late, corresponding to the end of the film 'Into the wild', where the young adult dies realising that we need each other. And maybe all of a sudden, he did not recognise where he was, therefore experiencing a lonesome world:

"Where I'm lost and on my own
Left my best in the beats on this trip, baby
Just please don't leave me alone."

Lord Huron

Whoever this girl is, he certainly does not want to be left alone in this lonesome world. The horn that sounds in the middle and leads the song to the final end, is almost like a call or cry to return home, Maybe he is calling to her in his last plead. The horn gives a strong idea of listening and watching for something more important than all the world. I thank Lord Huron for sharing their vision and passion in a great pensive song.

"All that makes the woods, the rivers or the air
Has its place between these walls which believe they close a room
Make haste, ye gentlemen, who ride across the seas
I've but one roof from heaven, there'll be room for you.

The body of the mountain hesitates before my window:
"How can one enter if one is the mountain,
If one is tall, with boulders and stones,
A piece of earth, altered by sky?"

Jules Supervielle

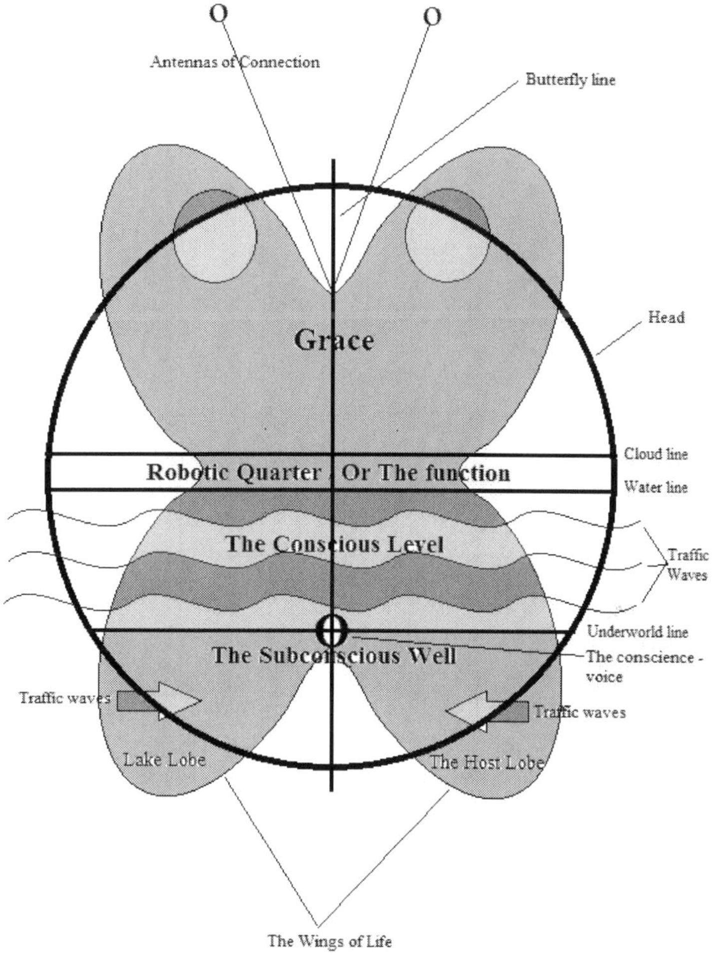

Influenced by the film 'Butterfly affect'

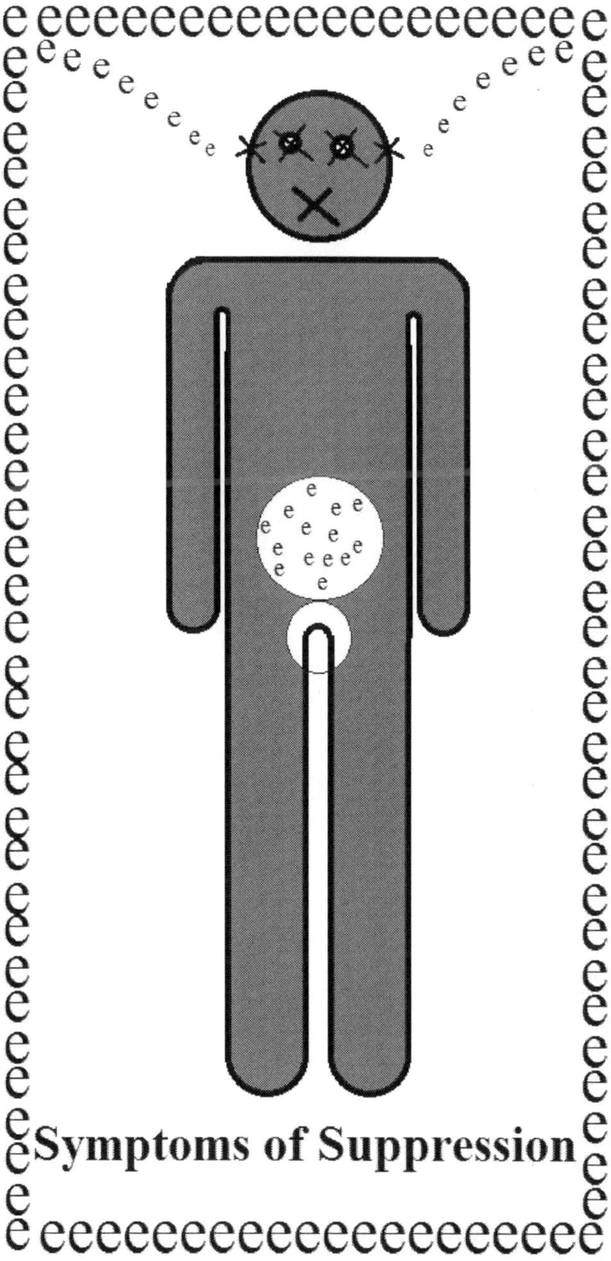

Symptoms of Suppression

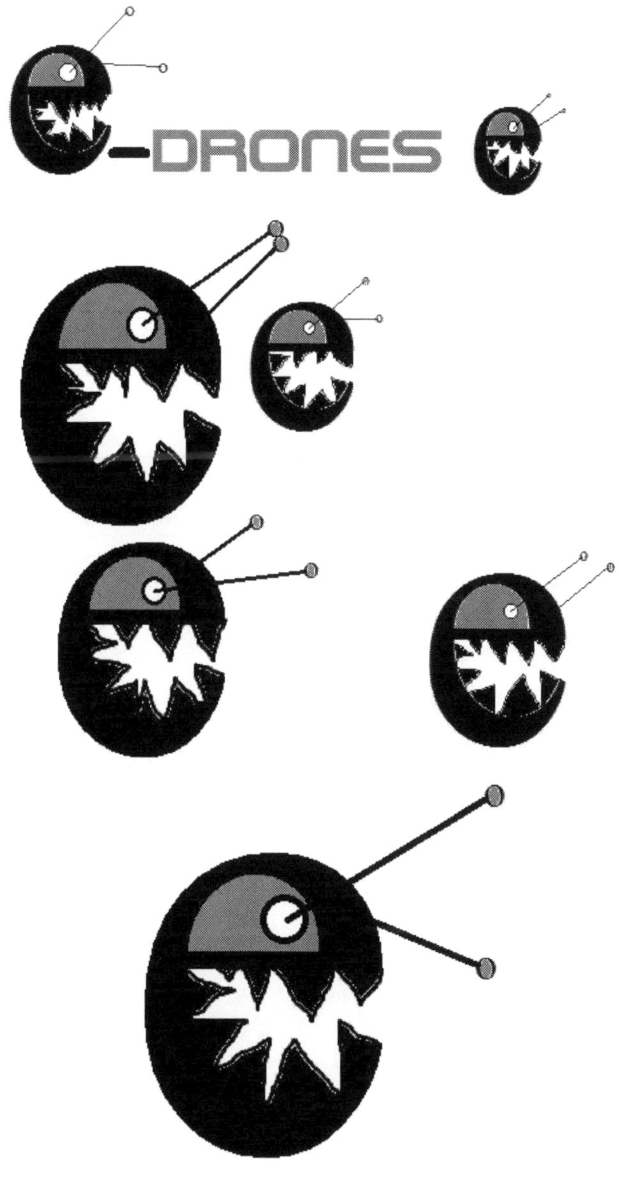
-DRONES

X
X
X X X X X X X X X X X X X
Caress me
Take me out
And fondle me
I am
Mobella
1 2abc 3def
4ghi 5jkl 6mno
7pqrs 8tuv 9wyz
0
I will entertain you

Two Dots on Either Side of the Great Divide

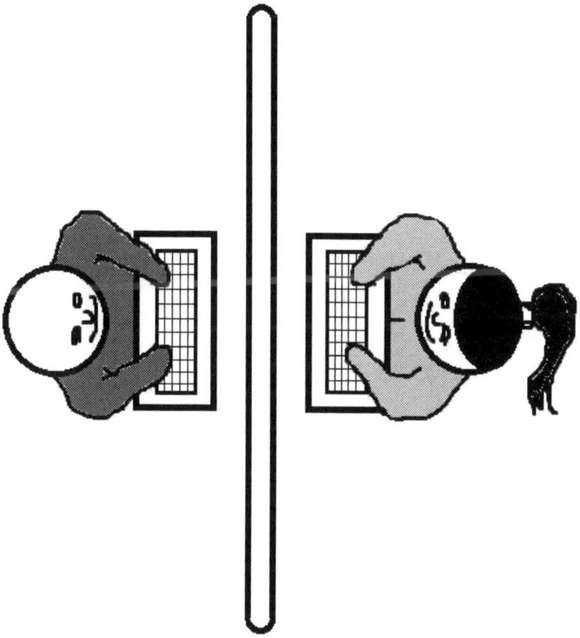

e-liens

Widow and Her two Sons

Mother teaching me everlasting
Or Father teaching me everlasting,
To death they part
Sing a song of dying
Burned out to make black charcoal
She weeps to this day,
Only death is proof to the everlasting
Has she ever been hungry?

Cars fly up and down –
On the road side
With my Brother and I
In the hands of togetherness,
Falling chapters
Painting the confusion
The panic attack of cars attacking.
There was no more cotton wool buds
Chattering of echoing breaths
As tears cannot be changed
We are just stuck on words
As my Mother speaks the images of pain
To stand and gaze,
Our eyes graze over
The walking unnoticed.

We could ask?
The advantage of still water
Runs deep its murky estuary
Its reflection shows double.

You stand there; there are two of you
Why should you go?
The haunting crows bitch
Screech in dark silhouette trees
That hack the evening sky.
A Black fortress with Silver gates,

The black widow spider is in envies
Clothes lay torn
Blood drips to the beat of time
Where the heart was ripped out
Time is ever so veiled.

The Queen Black Ant is eaten by others
Taken out of time, in the image of pain.
We lay down swords of hope
Shielding life, to the outcast.

Black grapes sit in the bowl today
As smooth as youth,
Tender
Or the bite of blackberries sharp flavour
Its twist to its appearance
Like the black birds lovely song.

For me you stand as the white widow
As the proof of love
Flows, like the birds,
Flowing around the sky lit blues.

Black

Black is a pigment –
To argue that, it is not a colour
Blame the sack-cloth filled with coal,
A chipped piece reveals a dismal glimmer
A slight glint.

Perhaps the fine dust of lamp black
Where it has built up its carbon particles –
From a flame
It covers copper to etch,
To sketch a scene
It flickers through rose gold
With freshly scraped gouges.

A clogged fireplace
To clean out the chimney from black soot
Where once a fire had warmed the room.

Black thread stitches,
To hem up black trouser legs.
A shortened occupier

Like a looking glass through black Pantene shoes
To spit on a shoe for a high polished sheen.

A leather shriek
As if a mouse beckons its voice to order
You can hear the authority of its squeak
A rhythmed eek-tick, eek-tick, eek-tick.

Does black stand for the shadows?
Or the clumsily blocks of dingy corners
The grey tones of old dusty webs –
Slightly blowing from the doors opening and closing
Or the people that walk by.

Is black the inward sight?
Or the body's internal organs
That is never exposed to the colour of day

Is black turning out the lights?
Is black pin-hole photography –
Allowing light to enter –
            For a picture to exist.

Oh Black Tulips
Are you a true black?
With your imitation with a pitch dark blue,
This deep blue of the night
Or a gloom of a dark hanging cloud.

Perhaps black water,
Like the depths of space –
Past the atmosphere
Where the lack of breathing harbours anger.

A Penny black stamp
Licked down with an underneath sting –
That hides a bitter tongue.
Franked with black ink
Allowing the letter to travel
Into the past, to the Victorians black.

Night Club

You could say labyrinth
Visitors in an Iron-trimmed fortress
One bar beats
Constraints me into,
Embodied solitude

Embedded,
Splitter hitting skin
Mind rather than body stood silent.
Conscious time
Standing and standing,
How,
Something exists.

Prevailing sounds and costumes of desire
Lights convict of silence
With eyes dandy for need
Hanging in midst of a classical illusion
My life's illusions stand at call.

What can I find?
Insert,
Insert to a changing you
Builds a model
Now imagine a model of you.

With certain hints of chat
Shoes of every ones fetish,
Controlling views of cigarette butts,
Broken glass.

Endorse the neighbouring body standing at large
To pass near them,
Making modifications
Aiming my way to remain obsolete
Encountering the abyss of separation.

Warning,
Potentially lethal lights bounce a trilling
Zapping eyes that flash fluorescent.
Consider a far place
To become the death of here

Equivalent digital impression
Take me away
I no longer want to be here.
Hours of thumbing beat
Beats me to estrangement
This is the confidential being.

The Day to Be

Friday 15th November 2002
(From, 'The Breath of the Dead')

The day to be…
Brilliant stretch of sky
A blue to be invaded by –
Office block, an unwanted closure
Coffins made up of paper and ink
Ink blots and runs to bear
The silent crunch in woods from sticks
Sticks, hear the way
A brush comes to sweep, skirmish underneath,
The echoing brush marks create a panic
For I hear sad thoughts falling bang hard
Sliding on harsh metallic,
The front of management
Turning rose wood into black charcoal
Black garments spread to each of us.

The day to be…
One for sorrow
To the magpie –
Knocking smaller birds from a home
The tree stems to below,
1904 to now
History made up only to be split into tears.
Screech nails on the black board
White chalk always fades
Drip to the beat of footsteps, leaving in silence
The day to be
Will you hear?

The day to be…
To be us, seeing strings dangling.

Alien Light

It was a humid night
The moon's round 'tiddly-wink'
Flicks into the air
Of a month's growing crescent
To a full open pot
Shinning in the dark, like pewter.

Oh moth fly, fly to the lunar light
And be free
Let your moon be...
What you hope it to be.

Oh follow, follow the moon;
As it projects its enlarger spot light,
In nights dark room
My lemon yellow moth of underwing
A natural organic spacecraft at the perilune.

Oh moth take your honeymoon
In summer's night of honeysuckle drift
For the moon will be your boon.

It is a little flutter, of a big effort
The moon sees him,
Beckons to lay and wait for a mate.

Grey silver
The lighting of white pith
Or reflecting silver blue.

I am drawn to the window's company
Moths distracted by the alien light.
So deceiving without any breathing,
Where you could dry-out behind the window
With the sun's magnifying rays that smite.

They flap and thud, then –
Through the opened window
A moth flies over to a lamp,
Or a kitchen light
Its silver grey wings of a dusty cloth.

One might fall into the washing bowl
Plates submerged in the water
Its small wings flaked,
Flouting like pencil sharpening.

Dust blows, and
Along the window-sill
Wings tied together like a bullet
Its old twig like legs stick out,
Like a Skelton tree in a desert.

Shinning outside is the moon
That is still prevailing,
Through the teasing window's sight
Moths Lured by tungsten or florescent,
The many species of artificial light
Its sinister invasion looms and –
Illuminates bright.

Oh moth fly, fly to the lunar light
And be free
Let your moon be…
What you hope it to be.

Oh follow, follow the moon;
As it projects its enlarger spot light,
In nights dark room
My lemon yellow moth of underwing
A natural organic spacecraft at the perilune.

Oh moth take your honeymoon
In summer's night of honeysuckle drift
For the moon will be your boon.

Mr Kiss finds himself
In a house party

(From 'Kisses in the Wind'
Loosely influenced by 'Willow the Wisp')

The evening soon came...
With the orange glow of the night lamps
Catching the drizzle

And the kiss slowly drifted up the street –
Passing cars and tall buildings.

Then a bus let out its sigh of exhaustion
To lower the step
    Tssshhh
A few people hopped quickly out
And barged passed –
Sending the kiss whirling around.

Moments later he passed yet another car,
Abruptly its alarm drilled into the sensitive night air
The yelling made the kiss jump and panic
So he launched himself into a handbag,
That belong to one of two woman –
That so happened to be passing.

The kiss rested...
Hesitant to look from his new found safety –
Twenty minutes had passed.

He heard chit chat, laughter and background music
It sounded muffled from within
Therefore he decided to take a peek
And like a kitten, his eyes marbled bright
As he looked over the opening of the bag,
His glow glimpsed around –
To find that he was in a private house party.

The kiss thought
    'This is great!
    I can mingle with the possibility of a partner.'

He floated over to the nearest girl called Hillary
To try and woo, circling around like a corolla
With his best courtship dance.

The kiss was invisible to people;
But she felt his presence,
Whilst drinking Vodka and Coke cola
Would she dare take a chance?
To investigate or give a glance
To make the kiss real
Where she would, to her lips feel;

But Hillary turned her back on him, and flicked her hair
And continued to talk with her friend.

The kiss looked around to see many cliques
Like the heads of hydrangeas
Where the fluttering petals blend in
To form clustered balls here and there.

It was exhausting trying to listen to conversation
As the kiss slipped in and out of consciousness
Comparable to the monologue reception of a radio
That has been interfered by a crackly hiss,
And whizzed up and down like an alien spacecraft
Then zipping back into frequency.

Oh, the kiss desired to retain
If only this muffled under water signal
Would be picked up by the boat's radar
Bleeping as a blip.

It was just the kiss's observation –
To see many people looking down
Staring intently into their mobile phones

As if no one was beside them,
Just the colourful lights that flickered
And reflected upon their faces
In the dimmed lighting of the living room.
The kiss just rested from trying to be noticed
Throbbing his breath as if a pulsar,
Just a dying hope that contained self-awareness.

The kiss had an odd burst of energy
As he looked around to try and get eye contact;
But his light of advertisement was not good enough,
So he continued to dim
Consequently he tried less for connection.

The music, the chit-chat and laughter
Was like a busy bee hive
Perhaps a river rushing over stones
Or a gust of wind –
That gives moments of loud rustles to the leaves,
All giggly and jiggly.

The female hands and arms –
Flapped around in conversation, all fidgety
So much so, that they nearly accidently hit the kiss.

Tiredness set in
This isolation had to fight not to cry
The kiss vibrates, wobbles and shakes like jelly.

Suddenly, mini black letters came from every direction
Instigated by people text messaging
As they were sent and received.

The kiss weak and helpless dodged the best he could
From this unpredictable bombardment.

He bounced on the floor
And rolled through the kitchen door
And followed the smokers outside.

The kiss tried to flirt with a woman
Called Nancy who was smoking;
But she just blew smoke over him
Revealing his form
Then Nancy gasped
    "Wow, what is that?"
A glint and stare of her eyes in a trance

Until her friend said
    "What do you think I should do?"
Nancy shook her head and coughs
    "What, what… What do you mean?"

Meanwhile the kiss shakes of the smoke,
Like dust or a blanket of soot swirling in puffs
He thought "That is it, I have had enough."
Suddenly he belted off,
An impulsive straight angle up
As if it was the spacecraft from the 'Flight of the Navigator'
He flew as far away as possible from the party…

e-drones

(Halloween 2017)

It is the letter 'e'
Where will you flee?
In this battle,
Where it seems to be –
Only me.

This letter is like a weapon,
Named e-drones
That are like repetitious clones
With their continues whine
Making prison zones.

Bellyache that ate all the e's
Bring a heightened sense –
To the ears of a sickly rave pitch
That shrills their sharp teeth
Like a bad trip Pacman specie.

Over exposed, to a white noise
That bleaches the sight
With notes out of key
Throbs a headache
Spinning the mind like a Frisbee.

It is the letter 'e'
Where will you flee?
In this battle,
Where it seems to be –
Only me.

Litter

I fear the pollution between us
This litter, this constant reminder
An eye sore on a beautiful beach,
It is this fight in the mind
That you have left behind.

It just lay there in the sand
A plastic container,
A false material dumped
And that is what I always see and find
Making me, to the rest of the beach blind.

The Day Time Moon

19.02.2016

The height of the bare trees
Blow in the wind
Silver Birch all thinned and rattled
Like a clatter of sticks.

The cold burns in the low soldering light
Cold; but sweat forms a hot flush
Temperatures clash, miss-mash
As the Inside of the body is confused with a blush.

Today the moon was out in broad daylight
Lonely in its dim light
Its dreamy science fiction –
          Celestial face carved into the sky
Chalky blue and a talc haze white
Powered in dampness, ghostly light,
As if someone had stolen the moon from the night.

The moon said "Farewell, I'll see you tonight"

In its haunted form, faded, pale and unwell,
As ET went white and said "be good"
I gazed and stood as if there was a slot in the sky
Pushing the ten pence back through
A dwindled silver as if spent,
As if the moon was miss-understood.

When it eventually became night,
I went outside
Looked up and said "Hi Mr Moon, how is the form?"

He replied "In darkness it is the norm."

The Thought of Cot Death On the Way to Sheffield

(With respect to my Auntie Susan and Uncle Peter, in remembrance of Nicholas)

Pylons stand in rows
Telephone poles, model like sticks
Refrigerator train is what is heard
Sitting looking from panels of glass,
Not a clean slate
For the grim seats shout public
Spots of repetition
Wobbling from side to side
A cot,
Carriages to Sheffield.

Trees stand in fields
As though they are standing –
In the middle of the desert,
Forms grabbing what they can
With their tentacles or fingers,
Arms to infinity
People fumble around, towards grey ideas
Infinity thoughts are aloud with pain
Slowly winding down
Not a movement.

The invisible mind
Dust mites a merge from old silent whispers
Back or side
Duracell batteries in wanting to recharge.
The last time I held this baby
Big bright beady brown eyes
With tinted blue vision of life.
His small warm heart
Beating to time,
For hearts never grow old
Not even bold
My mind exults to do so
Five to six years old, I never understood.

Jazz Poem (Sailmakers Arms)

With love to Hull

Horse's teeth chewing away,
Grass from your fingers.
Swimming butterfly across vast –
Improvised sea.
Birds' wings take on a storm.

My ears are carried, like my nose –
To the scent of a cooked meal,
Yogi bear, the nose of colour
Flowing him around
Splashed to please.

Woolly jumper marks the skin,
To unarranged sketches to Harry's face,
Lit with passion.
Alan Davie stands in recall
An animated vision of a drawing in jazz.

The lines never bear the vanishing point
Woodpecker to a hollow tree
Footsteps walk hatching the bevelled concrete,
A rhythm too many a shoe.

Palimpsest engraves many voices coming from one
Harmonising with fields of solid colour.
The blue moon howls,
Begs not to be a perfect circle
As Maureen runs her voice around
Like a pencil gliding imaginably over the opus.

Genus Rosa

(For Henry VII and Elizabeth of Yorkshire)

Prelude

Elizabeth has left him sprinkled thoughts
As if petals scattered before the King
Walking so proudly, in wanting to be with her
To offer her a wedding ring.

To have the honour in picking a delight,
From the bud, the petals astir, astir
She was a white rose that blossomed,
Where he will never recant his love for her.

*

The Red Rose of Lancaster

You can imagine King Henry's horse galloping
Clip-Clop, chop, churn and plough
The soil flicks up from the horses hoofs
Stern attentiveness with the scrunch of his eyebrow.

Thump, thump, thump, his Heart ponding,
Breathing heavily in passionate aspiration
As sweat runs down from his temple
Across miles, just to give his love a single red rose.

It lay there as if his bloomed heart
Petal bled of tender crimson tissue
A longing to always return to her,
She sings "Come back, come back, I miss you."

Could this red fire of lust be such a blemish?
On the white chastity,
As if the sunset of the sky –
Tinge the clouds with a red ant sting,

As the royal gala flairs in areas of claret wine
Making the heart giggly with surprised joy
Where perhaps her cheeks blushed
Like two children, a girl and boy.

Rustic copper shines its pink tinge
It shimmers in little areas in it lustrous pose.
The smell of a youthful scent
Upon the ancient rose

Powdered soft, like the fine drizzle
And the smell of Turkish delight
Made from the very petals,
Lazily flopped in a daze just by her sight.

From troubled stricken roses
Love takes a notion to circumvent
Their scents entwine in the air
Compose a sweet repose of disarmament.

Each music instrument, a saxophone
Accents of scent, a twang when spoken,
A song from the blackbird announcing –
That spring has awoken.

*

The White Rose of York

Elizabeth turns with a smile
And slightly looking down,
A glimmer and sparkle in her eyes
She accepted his proposal
And she lay down a 'Yorkshire White'
Of virginity,
Cloudily begotten in zinc light
A beautiful link from heaven's Queen
To the Yorkshire princess.

Behind a bridle vail was peace,
A soft face of quietness
Sparkles its delicate composition of transparency
Like tiny beads on the tips –
            Of standing threads of silk
Its softly flopped quilt,
As if the folds of her wedding dress
It shimmered its clothed satin
The ultimate hybrid in rosaceous.

*

Conclude

No greater silence is there, than after war
From the sight of the roses' armament
Cut deep the tender skin;
Blood dripped from the thorns so predominant.

But what happens when petals catch the light,
It glares its day time luminance.
It created the two counties to unite
As if catching sight of each other's countenance.

What flows in the spiritual gene?
But this combination of red and white,
Oh to live under the petal of serene
That ended 'the war of the roses' –
            In England's fields of green.

Now wild roses blow across England's landscape
The Dog Rose and the field Rose
I suppose you could say England's work force
With a proud emblem of the Tudor Rose.

From my Window

The dog must be inside today
Just scrape marks,
A small impact –
To the right of the door,
On the door frame as a matter of fact.

In fact, I laughed when I saw him outside
Waiting upon the step, Ha Ha Ha
Though his ego intact'

Or maybe to say his dignity
Inside with possible tooth biscuits
With calcium and other extracts
Watered and fed, all packed
And ready for a 'kip' –
        Without being in lack.

This mutt, mutters, mutters –
        Around grey in rain
Or a damp afternoon
In the yard looking around
Would he be outside at night seeing the moon?

Though it is always during the day
To catch sight of this dog
Does he need a groom?
Long strangely hair, small tailed
Pointed ears
Maybe a bit bigger –
        Than the head of a broom.

Sort of light brown, slightly golden
Like tea stains in a porcelain mug.
Woof, woof, please could I have a bone?
Or my dog bed, my throne.

The Sensible Snail

What sound does the snail make?
You could say stealth;
But yet his house upon his back
Not of great wealth.

No glamour needed
Leaves are their bread
And shells of swirling brown
With Spanish mahogany red.

Shuffling through the garden,
Their house growing as they grow
How economic! What a Den!

Closing his front door –
High upon the fence
Or upon the garden floor,
Or even on two pence.

I'm sure no ground rent
With his mobile home; what sense!

The Spiders Home

Sure, silver thread
Her peaceful web;
It must be the blue skies

Eating with table manors
She rolls her store
Attached to the Buddleia –
For the rain pour.

Web stretched from a distance,
Like light on the touch of the horizon.

Could you hear the spider?
Maybe at her size
Belay the rope,
A slight zip through the karabiner
And she dangles
Her optimism of an uncertain scope.

Spiders dew spun
Winter to low sun

It's not mystical or magical
To see the reams of a web;
But just optical.

A lingering mist,
Mini jewels of beads delicately attained –
The spectrum of light.

Letter about a Letter

As I write a letter
I think of the past few months;
To remember the best.
Though I often just write about complaining,
A visit to the job agencies –
And there is always some man who works there –
Is like a prop
Or support beam
Just talking to the women at the various desks.

Saturday nights are fun,
Static with excitement
So much so, that there are flames under my shoes
Maybe from my dance moves
Oh the dancing while heating my dinner in the oven;
But still, I fill the night with dreams
And wonders of the mind,
A few tunes and what's on the box.
I am exhausted with the cue of women outside my front door,
Oh and the phone never stops ringing.

I write more of my letter
Then think, what right have I complaining;
But that's just a cop-out
To just pretend –
That this green grass is better from this country
Though my heart gets the better of me –
And I write about some sad news.

I could write about metaphors and colour
Page after page – Yellow is not shy;
But it is not intrusive,
Bright as it is
It glows soft as I walk along a lane
At the base of Knockchree in the Mourne Mountains
I was not alone with the rest of the group

Though I love to talk –
I seem to blend in with the scenery.

I stop from writing and think?
This is all about me,
So I write a few questions hoping to get a response
How are you?
Or what are you up to? Etc etc.
Writing can be a tennis match,
Playing back snap shots of each other's lives
Blasted by with no return.

Handwriting, how beautiful
Just to have their signature in continuous flow,
Motion.
Hang on a minute, she has not responded – why?
I think to myself –
'Another excuse to complain, Excellent!!!'

I stop writing to make tea
And to ponder for ideas to write more.
I could write about my Brother's family,
My Mum –
Or 'Joe Blogs' up the road
Actually…
I have not written about myself in the way I would like to
If I had a job –
I might have something to say;
But who wants to hear –
That someone hangs out at their local job centre.

I never write about my garden;
Yet it holds great detail to admire
Brushing my pen
With soft melodies of spring.
I would not otherwise hear the soft sounds of insects,
The buzzing and rubbing of wings –
In a small world of joyful dance.

My letter comes to an end,
Though it is like a blog or diary
As I have not heard from my friend for a while
At the farewell my heart pauses
And I do send her my love.
Sometimes I send a few photographs,
Then with a kiss of approval –
The taste of gum with the envelope seal
And the stamp
It is posted…

There, done and dusted.

'What Language Does a Child Cry In?'

(Title copied from the book by David Hughes about Alice Sahhar's life)

Listen to the tears, rain looks –
As if...
Curbs flow like brooks
That fill and swell
Tis but one language
The sky that will tell.

Apparently it is summer
Where are the meadows to walk by?
A flimsily attempt to shelter –
    My umbrella to fly,

Flip flop, all inside out
Tis Dick Dastardly and Muttley's umbrella

It's not being wet
As in blue bottle blue;
But there is a chill –
Of the winds tail
That lashes and whips
As the roads flood and fill.

Cars drone
And splash on by

Where can you see a welcome?
Not from the buses glow
All stuffed and steamed up
An odd cough and sniffle.

Not from the Cafes' bustle
From dripping umbrellas
And shouting orders –

Of teas, coffee and hot chocolate.

Rain floods inward
Grates, pipes
And from guttering
Splashes and taps.
Drips from scaffolding
Or from high rooftops,
Even from hats and caps.

Drips from a nose
And pink wine cheeks,

Ping sounds on bottles...

Window panes quake
With channels of many streams
That reflects upon my room wall
Like stains that run in blues and light
To seep, swell and bulge
A round softness with dance
That races with some slow barges
Or ones that join and roll together.

Andcing

Based on West Coast Swing

To convolve in a finger print
Is it a crime to be in the mind?
The subconscious hold
The senses touch
To share, like a nut and bolt
Screws to tighten the hold.

From the anchor step
Six to eight
Lifts to the convex,
The branches arm
And in its apex
Leaf's fluttering wave
Twirls with the wind.

A gentle framed wheel
For the spokes
The cycle around
With the tires constant kiss
The grip, the wheels lip.

A Georgian key handle
Flicks with a slight curl –
In the middle
It bends, points to the other sides contact
Like a magnet pulling wire wool hairs
Lifts, like the moon lifts the tide

Draws towards
Warm towards
Draws out a splitter
It is sore to brush over the skin;
But warm water
As the leaves absorb to hold the sun –
For energy.

Love's Finger Print

Before

Finger prints transmit together
In an invisible world,
A unique form
On top of each other
Its intimate print swirled.

Press on this design
Identities ink
Around it furled
To be…
So tightly, its contours curled.

His finger prints hang around
As if he is unnoticed
They gather on light switches,
Turning out lights –
After they have been turned on.

I don't know whether her finger print touched his
Over laid with a hidden desire for each other
Where forensic scientists are trying to catch –
Their crime of love.

His and her finger prints –
Could have pressed up against each other
On a lift button, "1st floor please"
Swirling in a round bed,
She must have used the elevator ten minutes prior.

Their finger prints could have –
Met and picked up the same CD
(In a music shop)
Convoluted together on the case,
A mini dance floor prop.

After

Finger prints transmit together
In an invisible world,
A unique form
On top of each other
Its intimate print swirled.

Press on this design
Identities ink
Around it furled
To be...
So tightly, its contours curled.

Do I need to see the fingerprints?
Touched with affection
Do you tread carefully with me?
And wear white acid free conservation gloves
As they admire its age and story
Perhaps an attempt for an amendment.

People come and people go;
But their finger print remains
Where you had once been
Shall I dare clean the door handles,
Even a mug with your saliva –
        Where you had drank tea
It stands unwashed,
Glowing its energy at me.

Where love usually leaves her fingerprint –
        Invisibly on the heart
Where it hurts from your absence
You touched it, oh so many times.

The Ant and the Princess

Based on Rapunzel
Influences include Robert Smith from the Cure, song: Forest

These calls to long for, to search
To hear 'My Love, my love where are you?'

Wondering, dodging to avoid –
People walking
To be squashed and stuck to a soul of a shoe.

Sure, let's hide between splits
Or concrete slab lines;
But don't walk on cracks
To slip through,
Running between footprints,
Between shoes
Every one moves at different paces
The Ant runs as fast as his little legs can carry him.

Suddenly –

His antennas drooped as he is escorted
To the town hall
Does the judge call for the mare?
Scooping him up to put him in a jar
Then setting him upon a chair.

The magistrate peering over his glasses
The table to chair
No bigger than a one pence piece
Bronzed, brass and bare.

Like a bad penny always turning up
And rolling in
Or an autumn leaf
That has blew of the street.

Have you ever smelt that wood?
Smells like pepper
A poor man's teak
Well warn this court room
Bums on seats create erosion
Wood glows like honey and sap, this oak
Her medullary rays
Soft this thought,

Then –

The judge shouts
Nearly at the top of his voice
This judge to adjudicate
With his robe Prussian blue
Sequenced with silver around the trim
That shimmered.

Pointing and wagging
A Cowboy's 'second' hand of time
Colton nods every instant
The judges' finger rhythm.

He shouts that much he blows the poor Ant of the chair
Splatting him on the back wall
Sliding down like a cartoon character
Dizzy, spinney and shaking his head,
It takes a moment for the Ant to come too.

The magistrate tells the Ant his judgement
Suddenly the Ant escapes under the closed door
Then past shoes and stomping feet,
He nearly gets walked on!

'Phew'

Whipping the sweat from his brow
He decides to run to the forest
Following her voice that called to him

He heard it from the court room
She called
    'My love, my love, where are you?'

She was at the other end of the forest in her castle,
An adventure to get there.

Leaves are like tents
A fight through the blackness
Fiery red Ant with zest and sting to life
Rather than life to sting
Not a fly with wings;
But just the common black Ant.

Dark and damp,
Dangling lines and streams
Powdered like lime-scale and clumped white
A Network fungi
How about brown truffles?
Mushroom stools,
Velvet green moss catches droplet jewels

To scamper over old chipped and flaked bark,
Broken lichen covered branches, with old roots
As if hairs of a wiry curl
A distant telling from this dark.

Light swords through the trees
A hope and his determination –
Carries the Ant through
To the fairy-tale castle.
A classic single cylinder, like a final
Erected from the main building
And of course she was at the top
Leaning eagerly from her window
With long hair blowing a waterfall's sparkle
Singing those words
    'My Love, my love, where are you?

From the Arrow terrace and Crossed windows
Shall he dodge what is fired and hurled?
But the archery does not see the knight
And wonders at all the panic –
        Not a sight.

Running through the gap at the bottom of the door
No draft excluder
No tight squeeze
Big wooden doors, panelled
And gothic arched.

She was a giant to compare
The Ant looks up and replies back to her eagerly
        'I am here my Dear, my dear; I am here!'
She looks around puzzled?
She did not see the Ant,
Expecting a knight in his shining armour
She repeated
        'My Love, my love, where are you!'

'I am here my dear, my dear; I am here!'

Hearing the voice coming from the floor
A peep from his mini world
She looks down and picks him up –
To the palm of her hand
Squinting her eye she thinks
'That is a funny looking insect!'

No, No he said
        'Here I am my dearest and truest'

'Where is my love' she cried and sobbed?
She was soft and kind
Set him on a piece of paper
Opened the window
Letting the Ant glide back to the forest

As she Cry's 'where is my Love, my love'
And the Ant always in return
          'Here I am my dear'
His small squeak of a voice vanished first
While her voice prolonged
As he flutters and glides to the ground
Holding on tightly to the paper,
Sailing on the winds tide
The Ant suddenly remembers the judge's last words...

The paper vanished from her sight
As she continued to cry –
          'Where is my Love?'

Blank

These For-get-me-nots
Leave me in many knots
They are of a lovely blue,
Small and petite with a dot
Dotted with a yellow and white star
The petals like water drops
When there is a group, polka dots.

This busy fleet
Who shall there be to greet
Or who to meet?

Chess is out of the question
Cog wheels and black smoke,
Just to choke

What a weed!
You could still put them in a vase
To say,
  "For-get-me-not"
I forgot what I went upstairs for,
To be 'Winnie the Pooh'
The writer must be in bad form
It's even difficult to fill in forms,

Words like swarms,
  Busy
A jumping knowledge of nothingness
What is this, a Bridget Riley piece?
Give me a colour sheet.

It's not a blank canvas,
These For-get-me-nots –
Have so much character
Just to say,
  "For-get-me-not."

Insects

A Song for the Low self-esteemed

Try not to swallow me on your bike
Cycling in the wind
I might have been in the bin
Or worse still, on shit!
Especially if I am a fly.

I could get caught in your hair
If your hand brushes me away, I'll sting
After all I could be a wasp.

I might have one hundred legs;
But don't look at me different
After all I might have eight eyes.

Put a rock on me
Place me in a shady spot
I could have a shell or armour
What about jaws like giant tweezers?

When I am walked on, puss emerges and seeps
Sometimes an awful smell
Maybe a crunch, crack or squeak
Comes from, maybe a shell.

I could have wings that are transparent
That hums and beat to hover
To dance with straight angles
Then to land and flick my legs.

Around you, I may hover
Then a frantically waving hand,
For who could bother
A quick duck, a sharp move
A run for cover.

If I was a flee
I would hitch a ride
Live in your warm world with you;
I'll try not to make you itch.

Symptoms of suppression

(For those who suffer from anxiety disorder)

My eyes drift asleep
Suddenly…
A thud,
          I wake
Then again my eyes close,
I am sure I will fall asleep this time
A thud,
          I wake
It is like a nightmare, this constant waking up.

My head lay on the pillow in night's shadow
My lungs form tight
My eyes shut down, like a shutter of a shop front
Heavy and locked in a dry sting
Then…
A thud,
          I wake
This is too coincidental
So I try to picture and dream
My eyes are in comfort with my inward sight
Then…
A thud,
          I wake
My CPN said "how do they know when you are falling asleep?"
Even when I am asleep
Bangs and knocks over my inner child,
Or a subconscious voice
It is no beauty sleep
My breath slowly lows, dims in shallow compulsions
As if sucking out the air from a balloon,
Its staleness lingers in stillness.

Then…
A thud,

I suddenly jump out of my sleep gasping for air
As if from the depths of the water comes first life of breath
Maybe somebody gave me a resuscitation,
An internal kiss of life fills the respiration system.

My heart races from the panic injection
Pounding like rave music
As if it is running to get out through my mouth
I check my pulse, will I drop dead from the lack of breathing?

*

Vision

Jumping vision is bright yellow to green
Its sickness spell
Like the noise or snow of the tv screen

Its quick pins and needle dashes
The energy races, like thousands of twinkling lights?
Or the light flashing in the corner of my eyes

Throbbing its shutter in a film camera box
Or a dying pulsar.
Maybe car blinkers and hazard lights flashing on both sides.

Spare me the trickery
Black and white are dazzling
This Op art vibrates its visual hum.

Looking at pink polka dots moving on a conveyer belt
Its dizzy and moving imprint.
The small black words jumping on a white page
Just to read the same line twice.

*

IBS

Knots tighten in contractions

These cramps twists like a cloth being wrung.
Gurgles, flatulence of long gusts
Builds and combust
Sharp as a knife puncher
Wind moves with small bites of nipping –
And gnawing pain of nauseousness.

An electric shock in my stomach
It's pushed down
As if squashed at the bottom of a rucksack
Clothes neatly rolled tight, as if in the army.
You can feel its weight on the lower abdominal system
Further still, like walking on the hose pipe
Cutting off to a dribble
As if an isolated nunatak,
Through the snow as pale as my white face
A glimmer and glare,
As I just stare, a realm of space
Between sanity and insanity.

*

Tension

This constant clench
Like a block of wood held in a vice,
Could you lower the car from a jack?
To relax back on the suspension
I just wait, just waiting, as if my car to hijack
It is the anticipation.
Expecting that thief, in my home to ransack.

Could I be Frankenstein or a robot with a stiff wobble?
It's clumsy, as a fighting tense stomach,
Taunt in its stretch as my muscles try and swim supple;
But I am gasping as if in a swimming pool
Trying to front crawl, undersigned, uncompromising
An elephant in an atmosphere of water.

Then for hours the shrills, and sonic high pitch –
Of a tap being left on, a setting just right for a hiss
An infestation of a tight and tired –
Groggy, drunk and forgetful head
So I lay, heavy as a rock, dazed in bed
An elastic band tightens around my brain, pulling my ears.

*

Nerves

Defibrillator brings my body from my sleep
This shock of passing many volts

Like the hooped blade from the ban-saw,
Silver rust, it has a kink

Suddenly SNAP, it recoils of the wheels viciously
It has a metallic electric flick, a clunk
A thud, a loud fear
Where my arm and hand jumps back.

A small wooden hammer taps on the knee,
My leg kicks out
Then a snort, like an oink of a pig.

A pounce or a tug from a cat –
Onto a piece of string
The paws unleashed with its grip.

The twinges of muscles and limbs
As if I have the magpie's nerves,

Twitching and flickering from possible overhead danger
His sudden jerk down, throwing his tail up in the air

A shadow appeared, his pulsing wings.
The neurologist took the magpie of the list.

I am Going Out With My Computer Tonight

(Influenced by 'The Trashcan Sinatra' Song 'How can I apply to you')

The sun makes what I am looking at gloomy
It is plastic grey and dismal, in lonely silence
As static crackles to a wary touch,
On an old TV screen
It clicks, crinkles and pricks,
A rush that flickers a dull blue light,
As if the noise has sparkled my fingers.

Its solitary boring stare,
As if being switched off.
To be framed in a screen
The dark glare of a black reflection,
The backlight gleaming back at me
This screen dulls my look
Disheartens an empty desire

As –

"I am drawn to the window's company
Moths attracted to an alien light"

As the ball of my finger flutters its glide
On the window –
Trying to get contact with the other side,
Two dots on either side,
There is no getting away from the great divide
Long division only shows the distance
Where two worlds can never collide.

My key pad on the lap top,
A snap, click or a tap
With the my finger tips
That brush and slip
As if to stroke and pat.

I am going out with my computer –
Tonight
The lonely glitches of life,
just in the rolls and scrolls
of my computer's life.

To type a message to try and get contact
With the other side,
Long division only shows the distance –
Of two dots on either side of the great divide.

As –
If to flick through a bird book
Looking for that rare bird
Wanting to be there,
To see and hear the bird's grace of existence.

Sightings at recommended locations
With certain particulars
The condition and the habitat must lay right,
Its trees and positioning.

These binoculars seem to give a good sight
Glared intently at every slight rustle
Perhaps a flicker of colour that is garish
Its brash appearance ghosts through the trees.

Though the bird's loud colours call for his mate
Only the brightest participants win.
Insolent, cheeky and flirting tweets,
Messages of great song.

Can it be mistaken?
For other close matched birds
As if to distinguish
A Fieldfare from Redwing.

What about to compare

A Song thrush With a Mistle thrush
Its likeness is so similar,
I am undecided what bird it is?

The deciding comes down to pacific details
Of the colours plumage
And I wonder…
How to attract certain birds to my garden.

I am going out with my computer –
Tonight
The lonely glitches of life,
just in the rolls and scrolls
of my computer's life.

To type a message to try and get contact
With the other side,
Long division only shows the distance –
Of two dots on either side of the great divide.

Ego bulging muscles
Intently pop-eyed
With so many job vacancies
For you, for you, I have applied,

Where I sensed or knew at a glance
To Message my back-to-front efforts
Where I am sure she has had so many applicants
And I say to myself "Well tried!"

Next time shall I dare, lie or exaggerate on my CV?
Just a little fashionable enhance
As firmware rebuilds some replica.

I am going out with my computer –
Tonight
The lonely glitches of life,
just in the rolls and scrolls
of my computer's life.

To type a message to try and get contact
With the other side,
Long division only shows the distance –
Of two dots on either side of the great divide.

I am part of the unemployed race
Then I read "Don't really do unemployed"
Such distinctions I must face.

Perhaps imaginably they have been going out –
A year or two
He could have lost his job
In this dam recession
And all there is to do, is sob
You could re-write your wedding vows
Or simply, the bank to rob.

Years later a police man on the beat
It is your, now, husband
He is arresting me, as I am such a yob

I was just something that crept into your handbag
As a thingumabob
Oh that's –
Your phone lighting up and vibrating its throb
And, oh it is a message
From that young foolish squab.

I think of a Nirvana's song 'Come as you are'
But there again I have not met you
So I think 'type as you are'
But it does not travel by foot
As if from afar.
It connects you as if next door,
So close; but yet so far.

Normalrella Blues

Splish splash splosh
These shoes are well worn and torn
Walking through this puddle
To slip and slide
To fall through to the other side.

To meet in a place
Where we could talk
Or a little bit more like a kiss;
But this the place
I dream of your beautiful face
Dreams are made of landscapes
Where you are my secret place.

Splish splash splosh
I'm not sure –
If I've got on the right shoes?
Just the other side reflected –
To the skies blues.

To meet in a place
Where we could talk
Or a little bit more like a kiss;
But this the place
I dream of your beautiful face
Dreams are made of landscapes
Where you are my secret place.

Splish splash splosh
Frizzy
I like to see the fine braches wave
Set the silhouette –
In little lake caves.

To meet in a place
Where we could talk

Or a little bit more like a kiss;
But this the place
I dream of your beautiful face
Dreams are made of landscapes
Where you are my secret place.

Splish splash splosh
The sun dries –
To close the puddle's sight
And all I can do –
Is dream to hold her tight.

Whisper

Where can I even shake the dust –
　　For her to sneeze?
From in between
In a vacuum of a breeze.

The words that she shapes –
　　From her lips and mouth,
The wind of vibration –
Hums still water

And from the wind's stream –
　　Moves a leaf's sound wave
Its rustle tickles
A soft whispering wish in my ear.

Its whistle and wisp –
　　Of coming to a boil
A puff, to blow across the hole of a flute
The buzzes and fuzzes of the insects,
　　So minute.

The Milky Way

The spongy milky way
Though just debris
Of old rocks –
From a galaxy far, far away.

Is that a flying saucer?
Just one bounced off the wall
In such an affray.

Pebbles on walls
This space design of a house coat;
Shedding his white pebble dash
And I am brushing it up in a flash.

How about the stones in tarmac,
Glitter and flicker in evening stars
Like in winter frost.

The spongy milky way
Though just debris
Of old rocks –
From a galaxy far, far away.

Simmer

A big pot of stew, it was filled
As I brought it out of the fridge
Made two days ago,
        It was pretty chilled.

I placed the stew into a smaller pot
Sure, at low heat it simmers
Would there be –
    A puff of steam?
Like a shot
A burst,
        'Phew'
Like sweat beads from the brow
As a release of heat;

To watch over and hold
This pot that simmers
As a soft haze of mist, a smoulder to scald,
The steam that whirls and shimmers
Like silver and zinc white –
    With a low heat to fold.

When stirring Semolina or custard
You have to be careful –
        Not to turn up the heat to quickly
Who likes lumps?
Always gradual, to low heat

Who wants a burnt pot?
Just stuck, welded, caked and baked
Then to use wire wool or a Brillo pad
Scrubbing and rubbing,
    It is not a gentle dab;

To watch over and hold
This pot that simmers
As a soft haze of mist, a smoulder to scald,
The steam that whirls and shimmers
Like silver and zinc white –
With a low heat to fold.

Mongrel of Society

To hook and clip Tommy's lead to his collar
Is like trying to tame and lasso a wild horse
As he twirls around on the spot
Then runs eagerly on ahead, to set our course

He realises that I am not following
So he bounds back
Then in a second runs forth
I kiss the air to charm him to return,

"Come on Tommy"
I eventually clip his loop through the ring
"Stay, Stay! Tommy."
And it flicks closed the metal cling

Once Tommy realises that he is attached
His head turns and bites the mental chain
And tries to pull me along
As if he is taking me for the walk.

Could you say he was a tough man?
As if some kind of roustabout
This cheeky rascal
With his black and white oiled slick coat.

His territorial pissing can be just a few drops
Sniffing is his map of scent to scout
Then an unpredictable approach of another dog
Tommy's roust of barks, as he yanks about.

A woman walks passed with her small pedigree
She looks down as if he is a lout
And said "Oh God…"
From his session of a growling bout,

Tommy's fir on his back stands up
And he shows his pearly white teeth
The woman is in disgust
From him causing such grief.

Wildly so full of demons,
This time he was on the lead
Where there is nothing I can do –
To make him take head.

A monster when off the lead, as Tommy attacks
Then a squeal from yet another perfect dog
The woman hits Tommy with her stick
"He should be locked up" was her apologue.

My dog surely should be autistic
With his sensitivity to sound
A darkened blight
Lying ready to be found

The pelican-crossing beeps
Perhaps the phone rings
Or the alert of a text message.
Without warning the micro wave dings

Loudly disruptive,
A wild excitement of a woofing out burst
Our ears twist from the echo
He is always looked upon as the worst.

The growl of the rolling 'R's' Grrrrrrrrrrrr
Grabbing his rope then shaking his head about –
In uncontrollable flinging gestures
As if, he has wrung an animal's neck limp.

Suddenly he stops and looks up
The quiet eye of the storm
Ears pricked and twitched
Staring at me with two light brown planets

With a hint of a warm red
Oh turbulent Mars…

Eeyore's Song

"When you smile, the world smiles with you;
But when you cry, you cry alone."

It's not Winnie the Pooh's writer
Turning the page
With letters that tip and pour
As he slides down the tree
With ease
But yet; Eeyore...

Just to one side
A pinned tail
Drooped like,
How did 'Eeyore' fail?

Words written for some;
But yet, does not think
How many times does –
Winnie the Pooh blink?

Just to one side
A pinned tail
Drooped like,
How did 'Eeyore' fail?

Oh Eeyore, Eeyore –
Stands at his reflection
Looking to the floor

Tinged with blue grey
Do not fray
Some what may?
May have that gift
In the songs rift.

Starry

(For my great Auntie Betty and Uncle George)

Oh put a note on a shooting star;
But how I'm I supposed to put the rock –
        Back in the air
Maybe attach it to a rocket,
Or a fire work, to send my letter –
        In a flair.
Sparkles like shining stars,
Shimmering, like hints of a prayer.

These words to explode
To spray around my head,
As a child to be engulfed –
By a fire-work display.
Like a bucket of cold water
To splash around my face
Or the snow, thick cotton wool buds
Travels past as I look up,
They are all around me.

When we are apart or afar
And this vast sea is all that I see,
Oh be my lodestar
Navigate your heart to me
And look at the brightest star
Where I will be looking
And our hearts will be in synchronicity.

Therefore you are being missed
'Home sick' and 'Person sick'
Where Aunt Betty needed her husband,
As she paced up and down
And kept the bed side lamp on.

During a phone call from afar
George said

"Look out of your window
And look at the brightest star
And I will be looking at the same."

A star that can kiss and tell
Like a little memoir
Just a little of their life that shines in the sky.

When we are apart or afar
And this vast sea is all that I see,
Oh be my lodestar
Navigate your heart to me
And look at the brightest star
Where I will be looking
And our hearts will be in synchronicity.

Blinks at a flickering rate
As a heart –
Behind a blanket sky
Beats with sudden hints
Bickering who can be the brightest;

But just this one smiles
That twinkles and dances
Just to say…

You're the brightest star for me.

"Perhaps one of the best things about looking at pictures is that they allow you to glimpse the world through the eyes of someone who is not you. Why this is good I'm not entirely sure, although I like to think that it has to do with the relationship between escape and images, essential components of those imaginary worlds we need to visit regularly to remain sane (we dream in pictures)

Michael Raedecker

Imaginary Wife

I could imagine –

A rug rolled with caves,
Maze crevices,
Rolls of walls and Small hills
Through these lands of vast –
　　Carpet spaces.

I see a duvet
A plateau above like star wars.
Shelves as an evil base, towered
With books as automatic doors
That slid across to close.

Princess Leia and Han-solo
They met on the carpet floor.
They were not swept up upon the shore;
But he searches to rescue,
Worthy of Han-solo himself.

There is a lot to fight through
With various enemies
From jaws to giant claws.

The bedroom door was a boundary –
To yet another galaxy.

*   *   *

A film continues to roll
Here I am
In Belfast's rugged land
In county Down drumlins roll free
As green glistening marbles in rain.

Running as the running water…

I am but a warrior
A carrier of love
To send, to give.

The hero needs a rest,
To lay in his bed
I lay with stars that shine in evening dream
And all of a sudden I seem to be married
Hold tight now, to these dreams
To always make a great team.

*   *   *

Evenings in, on the sofa
I am mesmerized by her loyalty
Here she is!
A painting, if you like
I suppose I just call
We are inseparable…
And from the world around impregnable.

We could be a constant mating Dragon-fly,
Or she my damsel,
To be attached to form the shape of the heart.
It is in these knots that we tie

Always tightening our secure grip
Where we could never slip
Nor our love to deny.

My damsel is in distress
My aid is as prompt
As if through my enemies stomp.

Now she is in my safety
It is at a glance, an interlude to be shy;
Yet it is where we can be ourselves
While walking her home
In true devotion to testify.

This my Damselfly on the water's edge
I am him, who she looks for
That she has been longing for.
Before time itself,
Waiting with her transparent wings
Where the moon blends between light and dark
From the crescent, half to full
Flooding love's sleep.

Until love wakes her,
This the moment of urgency
To meet in a chance that no god of fait could control
It was the hope that brought us
To meet so close together, forever and ever…

Interlock this E-wok base
Its naturalistic realms
With splendid acumen
And with it being a great den –
For us to mate.
And Han and Leia are at it again.

Now rolling in the long grass
Is that a feather from a giant bird?
I could attach them to my figure

Like giant wings; but that is absurd.
Will the bird that it belonged to –
Return with vengeance?
My sweet, I must go to protect our home
Work is a security that I have not got.

The feather could be from the cuckoo
A nest under sinister invasion;
But more likely a giant Magpie
From their ever boisterous fighting.

A hero is always with his eyes open
Watching out for possible danger.

"Come back to bed, my dear"

What could I afford?
Sure, my love is as loyal as Star Wars dolls,
As I lay them together –
Princess Leia and Han-solo
She never left my side
I shall always confide in her.

We spend glad moments in evenings
"What did I do now?" leaning my head back
With scrunched eyebrows.
But then, just as allusive
And as quick, we have made up
And now frolicking on this sofa.

*   *   *

We always make it,
Though when arguing, I sleep in a separate bed
She could have just fled
And all that was said –
Is that, I love you

I'm sorry...

We could be the newly wed
Unpredictable with excited energy
To find our annoyances a charming place.
Each time we are even closer –
With the basics of bread.

"Is it time for bed?"

I shout in, with her already in snuggery

"I think so, my dear"

With a smile I leap into bed
And said "How about this Hero?"

She replies "You are my Hero!"

So ardently voiced.

A word of reassurance
That she is still there
She takes my hand –
In this treacherous land
It is she that knows me, so well...

What are you doing my dear?

"Just making us a cup of tea,
And maybe something to eat;

But I could make her
When she comes home from work
To greet her –
With dinners cooked love
Not a Chief of great delight
Just someone that is always there to meet

I walk home, only to be…
My feet are quite snappy,
Happy,
To think about my bed
Where she lays
Just waiting for me.

Are you coming to bed yet?
You look tired and wet
Take off those things
I am here, don't fret."

Her warming arm to cushion
This dark night."

Only the night before,
I had rescued her from a gang
That tried to bully and cause threat.

She calms me when I am in threat
Her soft words are just what I need,
Like a thread
To stitch this wondrous relationship.

My dream offers,
Or to offer her my dreams,
To be my dream
And in my dream.

It is that we are one
A perfect match
Not as soul mates;
But something even better.

I paint who she is
And she is never far
There is no separateness
Even when I am away
My phone call to my brightest star.

We are not of great wealth
As the romantic landscape is in us
Running free,
Hints of colour hits of the horizon,
As if the colourful dance in evenings glow –
    Is our hearts joining as one.

My dear you kept me safe through lonely nights,
As a Hero sets out,
Not as the tales of John Wayne –
Looking across the lonely landscape
With a lonely heart to tame.

The sublime is held in the heart
Activated by the paintings landscape
And my dream projects –
    Her as my landscape,
After all she is my imaginary wife.

Performance

Released from her back body tip
A web is sown
To show twinkling on a home

The light that dances –
On these strands
High above miniature lands.

She hangs on her new net
To make a stance
Surly it is a good view

Frighteningly bold
With black and white
And an alien face,

Or space invader block
Squared or pixelated
On a juicy roundish form.

She vibrates and twitches
On her long hair,
Beautifully arranged

Now strong and wiry
Expanse across;
Just seen glistening

Perhaps a fishing line
Left precariously
Like crystalline

Maybe even treacherously –
Stretched
And is quite optimistic.

She had two points to join,
Put up like a tent
Pegged in at a hedge,

Then gummed and silkily –
Stuck to the wall
On the other side.

A white thread line
In the rippling wind
As a home breezes open,

Filaments blow –
In silver light
To catch my face walking

Stretches and bends,
Tickles and brushes
Like a feather's touch

She certainly did not –
          Hide her home.

Warrior

This cat bathing in the sun
His tail flaps
"I'm the cat in town
And I'll sit,
What can startle me?
Or to make me run.

No dogs around
Just lying at the bottom –
        Of this pebble dashed wall
Trapping the sun,
A wind breaker
And I am quite happily seen –
        By the passer bye."

This sudden change
What could challenge such an animal?
To make him say good bye –
To make him shy
Sure, birds flap away;
But not today
Just this one persistent magpie.

Is it one for sorrow?
Or one for joy?
Is it the cat that is a toy?
As the magpie lands –
On top of the wall

Squawking, croaking

Chattering and bickering at him
As if friends had fallen out,
They had to voice an opinion
The cat said nothing, stroppy

Looks up, lazy and floppy.

"This bird is challenging me,
          No way!
I will continue to sit
Quite comfortable,
I will not flee."

Loud the magpie cries
The cat is a bit more dubious
And tries to intimidate his opposition;
But then this gallant, brave magpie
With courage –

Jumps down onto the pavement –
Beside the cat
          And gets into position

As close as paw to claw
To chase away –
This mischievous cat
He was not quite sure –
          How to respond

"Should I ignore?"

"I know the bird is smaller than me."

Maybe it's like,
"Elephants are generally drawn smaller –
          Than life size,
But a flea always larger."
          Jonathan swift

"I know that I am a cat
How can this be?"

He gets up to try and stand his ground;
But the magpie, surely

Was tough,

Surely, a family to protect
If to push the right buttons
Then who could stop,
          This new predator, now rough

This black and white warrior
Blacked wings like a shield and armour
Jumping forward then back
With his mini stilt legs
The cat wonders –
          Is it a bluff?

The cat has surely had enough,
          Not so tough
Wagging his tail in mid-afternoon's sun
Flapping and rolling like a snake
A slow rippling wave as he sat
          And in the end, he did run.

Now his tail is stroppy,
Not like the savannah's Lion
Held high his tail of pride,
Not hunting today
Not like a hunter's tail.
Swept low –
          In his stride.

"The bed became a trapper's cabin, or a lifeboat on the raging ocean, or a baobab tree threatened by fire, a tent erected in the desert, or a propitious crevice that my enemies passed within inches of, unavailingly."

Georges Perec

My Bedroom's Wilderness

Night mares of childhood memories

A shadow casts like a net to catch
What could be in the moons shadow?
What could be resting –
In the depths of the boat's anchor?
Peering eyes
More eyes than bullets in all directions.

The wave of goose pimples
Creeps and crawls under skin
Like parasites, infestations
Ripples to make hairs stand on end.

The damp with hairs mildew
Furry, not to stroke;
But to release a spore

This fear pinned me.

A curtain to draw
To stand alert,
In strands and beams
Of some light to pour

As a lighthouse catches sight
Or to chase away what may fright
Like snow upon a woodland floor
Carpets its torch
Illuminating corners,

To ease away this night.

Maybe my room is the lion's den
What lurks in the creases, in the folds?
And in these folds run more shadows
That creeps with the moon light.

Sure, my imagination runs away with me
Across the Savannah

Stampedes the wildebeest
The wind to stand at charge
Howls through
Dark blue.

The shapes and forms
From Jumpers and T-shirts
That are hanging over bedroom doors,
Are fears that appear –
Like a tattooed tiger's paw
Groping or grabbing hold of one shoulder
Ready to unleash his claws.
His face emerges, to peer over
With his tail whipping around the back.

Maybe clothes lay sprawled –
On the bedroom floor
Fashioned like a creeping cat,
Or deadly snakes and spiders
That move then halt,
As if a stiff corpse.

And spewed out from half opened drawers –
Is a clothing's arm dangling over?
What will emerge from within?

My heart thuds…

Maybe the sleeves hole

Or the dark entrance to the neck –
Of the jumper
Could be the yawning mouth?
It's rippling with shouting roars
From blackened teethed jaws.

My eyes have no rest
The visually sensitive
Did that garment move?
It might be closer now
Maybe I should get out of bed and prod it;
But its venom, it might spit.

How about clothes left –
At the bottom of my bed
At my feet, it could pull, tug and tare
From the leaf's curl
Shall my feet feel cool air?

Under the bed might be a hippopotamus;
But my mind is not that lucky
It is a crocodile!
Snapping its gape of ridged teeth
Oh, it's just my trousers left stretched –
Half under my bed, what a relief!

The bathroom at night is a long way
With glowing cats eyes, giant cats!
Or a spider's web brushes the face

Did someone touch me?
Or to my ear the fluttering of bats?

I run to the bathroom
Always on the look out
Then standing with my eyes to the door,
My penis, I am not sure, is it aimed right?-
"Mum! I've wet over the seat again!"

Now ducking as I make my way –
Back to my bed
And into its lush duvet leaves
Like peering from a cave entrance

I am safe for a season

The animals that lurk round and about,
Snapping and biting the air
With roaring rings
My curtain still ajar
Maybe to see the twinkling stars.

Premature

(For my Mum, in remembrance of Andrew)

A ton of weight
Hangs in the sky
Defies gravity
This black cover,
A laboured freight.

High up in the sky
Its weight in inches
It rained in an hour
What gathers to hold its contents?

This sky gives birth
Thin rolled out sheet of wet blades
The grasses dew spun,
Wrung like wet towels on a line
Drips freshly.

The water broke in her labour
A small part of a cloud –
            Is only impart
To the whole,

It is the mass
To the power that creates
Like the delicacies of the insect world
Pollenates to the trees crop –

As my Dad said, "He is perfect"

"Let me introduce to you the four walls: imaginary wall, hope wall, desire wall and loneliness wall."

Single

(The Daffodil trilogy, poem 1)

I am tired, to awake, in an empty bed
To fold and roll,
Sprawled, to mellow
To loll on my pillow
Shall I dream of these folds?
I shall, I shall
In Daffodil clear

To see this feminine touch
It's alright –
To tell me to hush
To lay in yellow and to gush,
A comforting sight
Is it needy to desire colour?
Its loyalty is bright.

1st of March, a Welsh memory
Rolled and bundled up
Heads closed, shut eyed
Two elastic bands –
        Hold tight the bunch.

They now lean on the rim of a vase
Green stems highlighted –
        By a sabre sword
Leads to its back paper scrunch,

As the petals stretch from a sleep
To meet gazing eyes
With the scent of being present,
        Brings a smile

I must consult in beauty.

When I breathe, I am free
In an outside wonder,
I could be on a spring walk
If colour could talk?
To answer back my complements,
My endearments,
Of petal droplets shaped in African shields
Like the dawning of Mother of Africa
It's circulated smile,
Ruffled and frilled
Like a hand to fuzz hair
To give volume, to scrunch

Or to roll like curlicue
Writes at the bottom of the hem
As frilled sheeting hangs from a bed
Softly pearls in skin touch,
Silk over skin
As feet rolled in a linen sheet
Or duvets warmth.

This yellow is better than a lamp
I know it glows in lights out room –
Of my living room
These walls as my tomb

They explode and boom
Splatting and flashing –
With sprays of a yellow bloom

To whom, does it give?
Or shall send in hope
Cut and displayed
To take away –
A hanging loom.

A night that hangs and covers colour

Hides its glory
Drapes its Prussian blue
Of its deepest darkness.

In shadow black
Eyes shut in daffodil bud
To open to display on hearts arm
This sleeve could wilt
For how long, how long?

Islands

It is concrete, just out the back door,
Vast to such a small creature
Running over huge boulders
Scuttling and scampering for cover,
It is an adventure!

I name small tufts of grass,
Which are Islands on grey
It had Dandy Lions
Therefore it was called 'Lion Island',
And it was over grown.

On another Island –
The grass was shorter
And two insects where mating,
Though I think I walked on them –
          By accident
So I named it 'mating Island'

On this old rough concrete
With a canyon to compete,
A crevice, or a deep cool ravine
And what a wilderness in this heat;

But yet it is where I walk my feet
On cracks in a modern scene.

A small twig, or a dried plant stem
          That could be a fallen tree.
Lying on this terrene.
With little bits of grit, stones and dry soil

I think upon the concrete as an ocean
With shiny stones as tips of waves
Sometimes it is the ocean that hugs –
          The small Islands set at sea;

But it is the small Islands of green –
        That hug this concrete
Softens its vast space
With lone insects.

He might bump into another insect
        As he hurries
Maybe an Ant, a spider or an earwig
This is the rush hour –
        That flurries

An insect like Silverfish,
A slither, a fine piece of silver
Cut in facets that move and bend,
        As he scurries.
He is smaller and hides under thin dry mud
It is cool and safe there.

How about a tree
There is nothing to compare –
        To an Island leaf,
Leaves like mini solo-panels
Soaking energy
Just like Butterflies,
And Hover flies sunning themselves –
    In the sun.

Needy

Tommy follows me around, as if I am royalty
It's no accident, my restless walking proves his loyalty
His need to be that close to me,
Like his flees he gives to me
Scratching with this unsettled attitude of being paltry.

Often in his cushioned 'petface' bed he looks snug
I put on the kettle to have tea in my favourite mug
To know these days of a lonely war
To burrow like a flee on my dog to the core
Biting with small nips of devotion, after all he did want a hug.

He wags his tail, dip tipped in white to write a note
Flickers between quotation marks to denote
His changeable mood
Not because he has no food;
But a need with in a hope, what was it he wrote?

"I am glad of your company"

The giver of flowers

Micro-organisms crawl where you don't see
Touches and inches my nose to sneeze

Terms and conditions
To use with money
The Puke on machines vending germs
Surely only flowers cause suspicion
As I collect my chocolate bar from the slot.

She the nightingale glides and sings
The patients love set before
Is he English?
If to bring a rose in time of pain
Its blend of beauty and thorn, mingles
Is it the ring of roses?
Surely it is –
To bless you, to bless you
Yet, she did not cause

How can beauty
(That touches the heart with joy)
Give you pain with the plague?

How about lilies to refrigerate and freeze
As Mark Quinn's eternal spring
To hold and heal
They still wilted, cased and contained.

This association with Lilies
Someone 'being' present, replaced by memory
A memoir of sympathy

The passer of flowers
The giver, to view
If, in a hospital bed
Surely gladdens the heart

The heart, I say the heart!

Could flowers deceive you?
If I on valentines
Should bring you a rose –
Surely, a tissue, a tissue;
But I want to bless you

The bad germs if I could wipe
What about a computer virus
To walk amongst the chips
And have a clinical key board type,

Like a mental virus

To smell the flower, the beauty to inhale
Maybe I don't want to sneeze;
But beauties scent to linger.

Would Kathleen Partridge Leave?
Without giving a Flower in the ward
The naming of flowers,
          Is all, but – Love
To send a bouquet note
Written in colourful blossoms.

I could be disguised in petal leaf drift
Like clematis climbing to bear
The 'Mental Beauty'
To form in the mind.

Would Daffodils trumpet germs in your sleep?
Breathing the sweetest scent
As if to be poisoned, invisibly deadly

Surely, bacterium spawns upon
Shit, piss and puke
Food left

Un-cleaned sheets
Used needles and bandages
Left used tissues,
Reheats and left meats

Is this the sullen pledge?
Is it the petal kiss?
A tissue, a tissue;
But I want to bless you
Or surely its basic hygiene that is the issue

My open wound
What will you catch?
If I send you flowers

If to lay a petal on a wound
Absorbs like blotting paper that blood
They call her the English rose
To scrape, to cut and scratch
Will it give a sore throat?
Or is it loves metaphor of the pain of loss
Hurts in blood red
Yet her beauty keeps

It's never a tissue, a tissue;
But to bless you, to bless you.

If it were to rain money?

Influenced by the album cover by the 'Mike and the mechanics',
'A beggar on a beach of gold'

This is a weather warning!
The forecast for tomorrow –
Is to rain money
It will last for most of the afternoon
Please stay in doors for your protection.

The next day soon arrived with people –
Peering to the skies
Waiting for this memorable moment.
Clouds gathered coloured, brass and copper red
Dance in the sunlight with hints of gold
Shimmering before our very eyes.

A single crack, the anticipation
Like hail stones that come slowly few, of four and five
Crack, dump, ting; crack, dump, ting
Shards like glass
The cling and clinks of drinks
Bounce
And then a heavy shower
A continuous – Da, da, da, da, da
Then, Drdrdrdrdrdrdrdrd
Crash, bang, clunk
Thud, wallop

People stopped what they were doing
Ran out of their houses, office buildings and shops
And proceeded to the door, to try and gather
To be bombarded with gold nuggets
Of 22 carat gold, mixed with £1 and £2 coins
With £50 and £100 notes in between.

They bounced off anyone who ventured out
Cutting people's heads,

Bruises and cuts appeared
Streets mingled with blood red
Yet, what was it that kept people out
In this coin fall?

Handkerchiefs covered gashes and cuts
Blood runs down eyelids
The mixture of joy and pain
Umbrellas soon torn and bent –
        By the heavy pellets of the coins.

Ambulances had to arrive
Because of people being concussed and badly hurt
By the violent coin fall.
The ambulances also ran into difficulties,
Broken windows, dented doors
Medics had to use metal sheeting covers
Ta,ta,ta,ta,ta,ta,ta,ta,ta
As they ran to aid the patients with the first aid kit.

After the coin fall
When you walked, crunch
The kicking of coins and nuggets rolled
I even seen some notes fluttering like a drizzle
As the streets grew quiet, a peace full interlude
Before yet another scurry of people
(The clever ones, which had waited for the coin fall to stop)

Crowds used buckets, boxes, trollies and all sorts of containers
Tesco 'bags for life', bulging at the seams
Jeff Capes would have been handy
Pulling arms from sockets,
If you had no belt around your waist
It was very hip hop
With coins packed into pockets.

From coffee shops, paper cups, mugs and bowls
    Full to the brim

Instead of bottled spring water, bottled money
Street cleaners came to hoover and suck up the coins
With its turning brush, instead of rubbish.

There were fights and squabbles
As people wobbled
    And slipped into each other
From this shimmering metallic surface

People crying and shouting as they ran outdoors –
    "That could help my house mortgage
    Or, my medical treatment
    Send my son or daughter of to college."

Was this an answered prayer?
Would food banks be closed?
The damage to buildings with most of the windows
Either cracked or broken.
What about old buildings, especially made from sand stone
Erosion in an accelerated rate
The conservation teams is expensive.

Cars riddled with dents, chips and scrapes
Small boats machine gunned to splintered wood.

The cost of the NHS with causalities and deaths

There was so much damage
The place was trashed
From all this cash.

Many people lost their pet dogs and cats
Animals, trees and wildlife
Badly ravished and shredded
Blew blades, branches cut
Severed, or axed
By this shard of gold coins.

Maybe if it rained dogs and cats
It would be friendlier

I wonder what would happen –
            If money could grow on trees
What would the bud look like?
Or what about the leaves,

Fruit would certainly be missed.

A New Super Hero Called 'Fartman'

(This was not an intentional copy; but rather "two great minds think alike." With respect to the original Fartman (1992) Howard Stern.)

The wings of a bird riding on hot thermals,
The heat and flow of the Jetstream
Is nothing compared to Fartman
He's certainly not silent with his opening titles –
And rippling theme.

Is he a good or bad fellow?
With his costume in brown and yellow
A hint of red for the belt
And his initial on his jest.

Pop-eye pops and bulges his muscles
Like Fartman's bloated combustion
Bulging to lift off…

His jaw is square like a box
Then striking a match upon his rough hairy stubble
He squats ready to launch
"Stand back everyone"
And sets the lit match under
"Ignition"
Fire sprays from between the Haunch

And the smell knocks out his foes
And off to the moon he goes.

On his return…

Fartman has a secret device
'The Whoopi cushion'
That he has stashed behind a pillow.

Then from his air filled body he thunders

"MY ENEMIES, I AM HERE,
COME AND GET ME IF YOU CAN"
His voice travelled miles from his winded bellow.
Some had arrived keen to give Fartman blows,
Fists emerge CRACK, THUMP and WALLOP
THWACK…
Fartman tries insisting his foes
"Sit down, sit down, please
We must talk and consider our show!"

His enemies slowly and gently recline
Then abruptly from the Whoopi cushion,
The air squeezes through the lips
With a stench of green gas billow –

WHOOOOOOF……

Windows break and curtains flap…

Fartman keels over laughing
Ha ha, ya ha ha, ha ha haaaa…

Will it whiff in this direction?
From the open lit fire
The heat increases, contains and prolongs –
Its linger
Hanging in stagnation
Just for his foes to hinder.

Meanwhile…

Back at Fartman's house, attached
To a giant floating hot air balloon,
Filled with his deadly stench of gas
Hovering high up in the air
To avoid his arch enemy Dr. Tomb.

Dr Tomb likes everyone to live in a gloom;
But if he tries

To 'BOOM' Fartman's floating balloon
It would cause a stinky typhoon
That affects only his enemies
That stand at loom.

In Fartman's kitchen
There is many Cupboards
Shelved with an array –
        Of stacked tinned beans

As he opens the doors
Cabbages roll out –
        And Brussels sprouts for his catapult sling
To fire and fling;

But if Fartman eats these accessorises
Then he goes through a state of being flatulent.

For an invisible gas bomb rolled and sent
Gassing out buildings by sending it through –
        The vent,
Knocking out the dealings of drug lords
Ready to send their pilled and powered swords
To venerable youngsters and adults
And if there is any left standing
He just catapults –
        His Brussels sprouts,
As they shout
        "Arrrh 'What a stink'"
From Fartman's gassy bout.

Furthermore...

During a raid
Under cover in a crowd
Fartman lets one drop
Hopefully it is not too loud
A silencer, they are the worst!
Rather than a burst

It is a google bounce
What direction will they smell?
But when Dr. Tomb is ready to pounce
He drops like an ounce.

Outside...

Dr. Tomb's men run for retreat;
But Fartman jumps into his Fartmobile
And from the exhaust pipe, he lets it rip
Up the street
Knocking out Dr. Tomb's passing fleet.

Mr and Mrs Spoon

Based on the old children's Programme 'Button Moon'

A rocket, done and dusted
Peering from a round window
Waving, then wobbling from
Side to side.

Was I a spoon to scoop?
Reflected inside, or
Upside down in silver aluminium
Or wooden and splinted in dish water warm.

Food oils keeps me nourished;
But washing up liquid
Dries my wooded head.

I don't feel new
Or ready to stir a mixture,

I go round and round
Like the plug being pulled
With the waters whirlpool
Swirling, like the old joke
Dr. Dr. I feel like a spoon
Sit there and don't stare
        "Sorry, I mean stir!
But once I'm in the pot
I absorb what I can.

I am still waving in the rocket
As I travel to the moon
A button seems lonely in the sky
Just a form;
But to walk upside down
From it being so small
Not much time.

I find it stitched into the sky
With its four holes,
I did meet Mr and Mrs Spoon!
Looking at the view of the quilt work earth
Embroidered in fine arrangements
The weaving bends outwardly
Like the back of the aluminium spoon

Shinning its best
With clouds in cotton wool candy floss
To whom in view,
Mr and Mrs Spoon

Stars are just sequences
Glued on to dark navy blue mounting board
The craft lit sky
As I say "Good Bye"
As I go to Bye-byes
The bed's dream of lies
And I lye not to count the stars;
But to wonder of the back lit skies

I could have been their son;
But they finish the day
By flying to the moon
What a romantic pair.

Back to earth from my head in stars
Knocked out in cartoon tweeting birds
I come too…

My rocket is lonely
Just like every dancing star
Flashing, reaching to earth in night's quiet sleep
Here I am
I am home for awhile
Hold me tight and don't let go
Don't let me go to Button Moon.

The Unnoticed Princess

It was the school's day out to a country park called Crawfordsburn beside the coast, a beautiful woodland with a stretch of sandy beach. Elzellia was just aged ten, she was excited and loved being outside amongst Mother Nature. Her friend Angela was of school today with the cold. Elzellia missed her dearly and thought "We could have made daisy chains and put them in our hair."

The bus of children were loud and boisterous, always wanting to be noticed, as each child yelped "sit beside me." "No, sit here." The screams of excitement and the talking excessively is like the sky filled with the chirps and conversations of the Starlings roasting on pylon cables.

Mrs Molly Gates shouted "Please be quiet and sit still, I need to take a head count." She blew her whistle and slowly the laughs and giggles soon came to a silence, as if the roasting Starlings had now took flight to a silent concentration. Poor Elzellia was sitting on her own, Mrs Gates said "Come and sit beside me?" The bus of children roared into laughter with comments "Teaches pet." And "Miss goody girl."

Mrs Gates now seated turned her head and looked up the isle of the bus and shouted "That is enough"

Elzellia twiddles with her hair and gazed from the bus window. Mrs Gates was a lovely teacher and she spoke to Elzellia, bringing her out of herself.

"I am sure you miss Angela!"

"Yes miss, she just lives up the road from me, last week Angela's mum took us to the park with 'Bell' their dog, it started to rain and we all got wet."

Mrs Gates took off her glasses and rubbed her eyes "I remember that day, it rained cats and dogs. Awk poor Angela, she must have got the cold from getting wet, I hope that you don't get it."

Elzellia rubbed her nose “No miss, I was wrapped up well that day like a fluffed wee duck on a river.”
The winding and twisting of the road and the bus filled with the children singing songs that they all had soon arrived at Crawfordsburn Country Park.

Elzellia watched from the bus window as the other children disembarked and waited outside, running and jumping around. The other down side from sitting beside the teacher was that she stood blocking Elzellia from getting up from her seat. Elzellia was fidgeting and bobbing up and down, until she was relieved as the last pupil of the bus.

Mrs Gates obsessively did another head count, while Mrs Pringle said “Please make sure you have your packed lunches with you.”

Eric quietly and discreetly brought out his mobile phone that was whispering and muttering in his pocket, which said “I am Mobella, lift me out and use me, I will entertain you.” Eric stood there looking down to his phone oblivious to the presence of Elzellia who was standing beside him. Mrs Gates caught sight of Eric with his phone, “Put that away or I will confiscate that from you.” Her eyes pinned sharp causing Eric’s style to be blunt as he replied “I need it, just in case my mum phones me.” He quickly puts his phone back in his pocket and kicked his feet on the cement ground and sighed.

Mrs Gates leads of walking the class to the grassy area just above the beach. “Keep close together and keep up.” Mrs Gates turned her head looking around “Chop, chop.” The class broke out into laughter from her expression. Mrs Pringle the other teacher smiled to herself as she walked at the back of the class making sure no one got lost.

It was a beautiful day, warm with a few white clouds in a blue sky. Elzellia took a deep breath and looked across the ocean as she walked up onto the grassy area. The tips of the waves glistened in the sun light and birds echoed from the woodland behind. Elzellia’s thoughts where interrupted from a sudden shout from Eric “Yipeeeee” as he ran off chasing the ball.

Mrs Gates scratched her hair looking around at the class running and jumping about, suddenly she blew her whistle and bellowed "Gather around class." Everyone soon came close pushing and shoving each other, "Ok, settle down, today you are going to pick your own two teams, which you will stay in for the rest of the afternoon."

Lisa twisted and turned on her feet and shouted "Miss, can it be Girls against boys?

"No, it certainly cannot. It will be one girl then one boy, until you have been through everyone."

She stamped her foot on the ground "Oh; but miss!"

Lisa was the popular girl in the class who was always picked first, and for the boys it was Eric. So they were both team leaders and started to pick through the class taking it in turns. The excited screams and shouts "Pick me.", "No pick me." "Pick me and I'll be your best friend." Slowly it became quieter as the pupils got picked leaving the weaker or the uncool children to the end.

Lisa alerted quickly "We will have Nathen, and you can have Elzellia."

Elzellia thought "Typical, the last picked, how embarrassing." She slowly walked over to Eric's team. "Though I am pleased that I am on Eric's team" and she gave him a smile next to none."

Though Eric stood behind covered by the rest of his team with his phone that whispered sweet nothing "I am Mobella, Mobella, you need not another girl." And consequently whilst he looked on the internet he missed Elzellia's smile.

Mrs Pringle was laying out cone markers forming a large circle as Mrs Gates announced that the first game was rounders' and Eric's team got to bat first. Elzellia skipped over to the batting area and stood waiting for her turn. It was a small racket that they used and Eric picked it up first and confronted the bowler, which was Lisa; she was swinging her arm getting warmed up. They both stared each other out; but Eric got impatiently tired from holding his stance ready and loosely looked away. Suddenly Lisa threw the ball, CRACK the ball sliced off to one side, Eric hesitated; but his team shouted "RUN" so he ran to the first marker. Lisa's team was well placed and they were ready with the ball to get Eric out.

Most of the team had a go at batting and it was soon Elzellia's go; Eric had already made his way around the markers to home. Elzellia had a good forearm and she stood lazily ready, this time it was Kirsty bowling and she flung the ball. Elzellia stepped back and gave it a good hard hit 'BANG', the ball whizzed high in the air, and travelled a fair distance for a child. Elzellia throws the racket behind her and started to run behind the markers while one of Lisa's team members ran to fetch the ball. Lisa was standing at the last marker and puts her foot out to trip Elzellia just when she was nearly home. She fell head first and skidded on to the grass, her eyes looked down; a close encounter with the insect world. She zones into an ant amidst the blades of grass, as she heard the echoes of laughter in the back-ground. Distant across vast spaces from its nest, out travelling to search for food, "I wanted to be its friend and hide away." She slowly gets up with a lump in her throat as she held back her tears. She brushed her jeans; but the green grass had stained them and her hands where all brown with mud. Lisa's team had already got Elzellia out with the ball being touched down at a marker.

Elzellia shouted out "Lisa tripped me over, they are cheating."

Lisa's eyes locked on to Elzellia like an Eagle "No, I did not, you wee tout."

None of the teachers saw what had happened, and said "Be more careful Lisa."

"But I did not touch her"

Mrs Gates then said "Play on." Elzellia's chin started to go up and down and shake as she walked of and sat on the side to watch. Eric also did not see what had happened being so glued to his mobile phone at the back of the batting que, whispering "I am Mobella, and I will keep you occupied." But he soon quickly put his phone away from all the commotion.

"Ok, that is enough." And then Mrs Pringle turned and said "Are you ok Elzellia?"

As a pin to a balloon, and a bluebell's drooped like swoon in an over cast afternoon, replied "Yes, miss."

Thirty minutes later Mrs Gates blew the whistle for lunch and the children fetched their packed lunches and sat around. Eric sat with his best friend Antony, and Elzellia sat with Nathen and Kirsty.

Moments of peace for the teachers as the children's mouths where full. Mrs Gates caught sight of food being thrown about as one flies past within inches. She turned to Mrs Pringle and said lowly "Spoke too soon." Bits of crust was launched at each other. Mrs Gates was furious and caught sight of Antony throwing bread. "Come here and sit with me, at once." Antony had to sit with the two teaches for the duration of lunch. His head flopped all stroppy.

Elzellia looked across at Eric as he was picking grass in handfuls and shoving them down Nathan's T-shirt. He laughed lowly with a smirk. Nathan turned around and said "stop doing that." Elzellia started to pick daisy's that where polka dotted around like bursting stars; she started to make a daisy chain and attached it around her wrist. "Oh wow, beautiful" said Kirsty and she started to make one.

The seagulls flew down to pick up the scraps from the edge of the group, in their confidant yet alert behaviour. Mrs Gates watched the Seagulls and then said "Don't forget to pick up your rubbish and take it with you." Her head moved around Looking like a spot light at the children as they gathered their things together. Mrs Gates did not miss a beat as she pointed to a piece of rubbish been blown by the wind "That is your crisp packet Nathan!"

The games resumed after a rest and the next but quick game was called 'stuck in the mud.' Both teams had to get as many tagged as they could within ten minutes, and if you were caught you had to stand still (stuck in the mud.) However they could be released from being stuck in the mud by their own team member tagging them.

So off they went running around, panting and puffing, chasing one another like cats and mice, dogs and cats. “Miss I touched him, he won’t stand still.” Eric ran past and tagged Kirsty to release her; but poor Elzellia who also had been caught stretched out her hands waiting to be freed from being stuck in the mud. The children just ran about her like ballet dancers as they dodge by turning, ducking and spinning around, or like ice skaters on a lake gliding by with such speed and grace.
Elzellia felt like a tree with her arms as branches standing firm waiting; but it soon bothered her and she retreated and sat down on the side to watch. Folding her legs she looked across at Mrs Pringle and smiled and sighed. She started to play with her hair and looking up into the sky, she was near the trees and wild flowers. A butterfly fluttering and lazily hopping from flower to flower suddenly landed on Elzellia’s nose. It just rested there, sunning herself, stretching her wings open without a care in the world. It was very tickly and Elzellia wanted to scratch her nose; yet she did not want to disturb this beautiful and marvellous moment. She started to smile.

“That is better my dear.”

She suddenly turned around wondering where the voice had come from. The butterfly had now moved to rest on her shoulder; but how incredible the butterfly repositioned itself back on Elzellia’s nose. Again the small delicate voice said “What is wrong? Why are you not playing with the other kids?” Elzellia went crossed eyed as she looked to her nose, blurry and out of focus, just the colours like a kaleidoscope. She thought to herself “it is a Peacock butterfly.” Then quite nervously looked about and said “did you speak to me?”

“Yes of course, you silly-billy.”

Then Elzellia still looking about, with her mouth hanging open said “I am not playing because no one really takes notice of me, so I wonder upon the small insect world.”

Elzellia scratched her leg and continued quite chirpy “I notice the insect world, small and delicate and many look strange and funny.” Then eagerly said “Am I strange?”

The butterfly fluttered back to her shoulder and said "No, of course not, we are all individually different."

Elzellia said "What is your name?"

"Charmaine, and what is yours?"

Elzellia giggled and hiccupped and said "El 'heek' zellia, I mean Elzellia."

"Lovely name"

Charmaine fluttered around like a loose handkerchief, or the blossom from the handkerchief tree, white and tender in its comfort said

"Dry those eyes
Why do you look so adamant up to the skies?
It is all down here on home turf
Individuals usually have no idea their worth
So just get back in the game
And call your beautiful name."

"Come on, you can do it."

Charmaine then fluttered of towards the game thinking that Elzellia was following. She was nearly there and decided to look around, only to see Elzellia with her knees pulled in tight to her chin, with her arms wrapped around.

Charmaine then started to fly back when Nathan suddenly ran past sending the butterfly hurling in a gust of wind, around and round like a leaf in autumn. Gaining control she raced back to Elzellia in a panic and landed on her hair

"Wow that was close."

She closed her wings then opened them again and said "Why did you not follow me across?"

Elzellia sniffling lowly said "Lisa picks on me!"

“Well, I am sorry to hear that, should you not report her to your teacher?”

Her silence indicated a nervous no, she did not want to confront it, and as a child did not know how to express or communicate her feelings to the outside world. To sulk is all that she knew, to become quiet or afraid to speak and less confidant.

“You must pick yourself up”

Charmaine fluttered back towards the pitch where the children were playing. While Eric stood stuck in the mud Charmaine flutters up to his ear and whispered “look across to the side, Elzellia is all lonely.” Eric looked around and saw her on her own, he thought to himself “I must go over after this game.”

Suddenly Mobella who was in Eric’s pocket teasingly whispered “No, don’t talk to her, your class mates will laugh at you.”

Then she said “Take me out of your pocket and look at me.”

Eric looks around and reached into his pocket to take his phone out, when he thought “I better not do it here, the teacher might see me.”

By this stage Charmaine was half way back to Elzellia when, this time, a ball whizzed past, the suction pulled her back. She flaps and flaps until she suddenly zoomed on ahead and past Elzellia “WWwwoooooooooooo”

She finally made it back to Elzellia puffed out. She sat back on Elzellia’s hair tired, the sun came back out from behind the clouds and she stretched those beautiful wings and like the photosynthesis of the leaves that absorb the light, so do her wings, giving her the last bit of energy for the day. Charmaine then said “Cheer up.”

Elzellia dejectedly said “Why can’t I be as beautiful as you?”

“But you are! Try not think whether or not you are beautiful, the important thing is to participate and just be yourself.”

Charmaine decided to tuck her wings in and pull herself back like a sling. She zipped of like a jet aeroplane into the middle of the children's game. At this stage they are playing dodge ball. Eric had the ball and was just about to throw it at someone when Charmaine flutters in front of his face

"W… Wh… What the heck,"

It caused Eric to hurl the ball in the wrong direction sending it flying towards Elzellia. At this moment poor Eric was frantically waving his hands about. Meanwhile the ball bopped Elzellia on the head, she gave a sudden yelp, and Eric then turned his head and walked across to Elzellia.

"Sor…Sorr… Sorry about that, are you ok?"

"Yes, it just startled me." She flattened her hair, where the ball had hit it.

Eric turned on his feet and was about to walk off, when he stopped and turned and said "Are you playing? Our team is winning."

A smile appeared on her face, more beautiful than the butterflies wings, colourful in its beam, she said "Yes, I was just taking a rest."

"Oh, we thought that you just did not want to play."

"Oh, but I do"

Eric stepped closer to Elzellia and put his hand out helping her up to her feet

"Thanks"

They both ran onto the pitch where the other children were playing and Elzellia enjoyed the rest of the games. The time was soon getting close to go back to the bus; but Mrs Gates wanted to take the children for a wood land walk to collect various leaves for class. She blew the whistle and announced "Please gather your belongings together, we are now going on a short woodland walk before returning to the bus."

Elzellia wondered if she would see a bird called the 'Dipper', which can often be seen here along the river that flows through the wood land. As Elzellia was picking up her school bag and cardigan she looked towards the area where the butterfly had been and thought "Where is Charmaine, I forgot to say thank you to her." Her head drooped and she trailed her cardigan along the ground as she walked slowly over to the class.

Eric's phone started to whisper in his pocket "It is quiet and no one will see, bring me out and look at me, I am Mobella." Eric was just about to remove the phone from his pocket when he thought "No, Where is Elzellia?" He looked around and saw her with her head down, He shouts "Elzellia, over here!" She looked up, smiled and walked straight across to him. "Hi", he reciprocates in his cool manner "Hey"

Mrs Pringle gave each child a bag for their wood land findings, Elzellia collected leaves for Angela. Some of the children played out adventures, and the boys picked up sticks to sword fight, the cracks and thuds of the sticks that knocked together

Mrs Pringle's eyes widened "Please be careful boys."

Though the girls were being just as boisterous and Lisa starts throwing small twigs and sticks at Eric. Soon there was sticks and twigs in everybody's hair. Eric teasingly threw some at Elzellia. Elzellia was certainly not going to let him away with that and started to hurl her findings from behind a tree. Nathen finds spiders and throws them at the girls; the screams alerted the teachers "What is going on here?

Lisa without hesitation stepped forward and said "Nothing Miss!"

They all finally made it back to the bus in one piece and with bags full of an impressive woodland collection, which was also all over each child. Mrs Gates tuts and thinks to herself "What are their parents going to say?"

She gave another head count as the children boarded the bus. She turned to Mrs Pringle and said "They are bringing half of the woodland home with them."

Eric sat beside Elzellia and they both talked the whole way home. Elzellia thought to herself "I cannot wait till' I tell Angela what had happened."

The Sound Track:
1. Daughter – Youth
2. The Cure – Just like Heaven
3. James – Sit Down
4. The Farm – Don't let me Down (Hooton/Grimes)
5. Acker Bilk – Boodle Am Shake
6. Whether Report – Jungle Book

Driving with the radio on

Are you listening?
Can you hear the beats?
Alone with you
In these comfy seats

See all the colours
Red, orange and green
With eyes closed
These things unseen

Look beyond the glass
And your heart will follow
The rise and fall
Of another tomorrow.

Poem by Tracy Chan

Pro-Rap

Rap originated from the streets of New York in the eighties,
A working class, or a black man's poetry.
Early chanting's originated from Africa BC and AD.
Poetry can be performed over music by speaking, rapping, or even chanting
It is rhythmed by accenting at the end of a phrase or sentence
Like playing the guitar.

What about the rap?
Put a beat to it
And you have a tap
With a bass line
And a 1930s cap.

Are you going to say –
What rhymes with bitch?
Well, these words I will stitch
After all it is an expression
No catch or hitch.

So what if my hands –
Want to dance and twitch.

Their influence
Surrounded by the drug and gun
They keep everyone reminded
That the drug and gun is sold for fun.

Instead of suits, its gang warfare, or war fear
No difference to the war the suits fight
With so called polished edges
Sniffing coke, a white man's dust
And their fetish lust
The opera is full of stage dust
From the angels, the angel dust.

Sorry what am I reading 'Poetry' or rap?
Or is it the way it is presented?

These pigeon holes that we have invented
Where rap is wrong
With only sex, drugs and violence
At least they speak openly about it!

Shall they stay silent?
How can you shout silence?
To something that is a growing concern
Shall we put on the opera rose tinted binoculars?
Looking at her fine voice and clothing
Christened white
Surely the hurt will bite
At the sight of self-righteous attitude
With your view from the gods
From great altitude.

Surely it is social awareness
From emperor Penguins
With the flames of the tribes
The luminous orange
Like love without the bribes
Each in our lives
Hoping someone will hear their cries.

Some rappers are anti-drugs
Like Grand Master flash
I am not going to fall asleep smoking hash
Or do you expect me to steel your cash
From that money that you stash
Did words come clean from the Clash?
The Rockers and Mods and their heads to bash.

Any way it is only how words are presented
Or preformed –
Through spoken word, Music, chanting or rap.
A'men…

The All New Revamped 'Metal Man', With Bumbleine's Love

(Influenced by Stumbleine by The Smashing Pumpkins
And the cartoon, Inspector Gadget)

A Queen bee is out in search for a new hive…
Her last colony was sprayed with pesticide
A cruelly intentioned chemical attack
That slowly soaked inside
Where she had to shrink back to survive
And now only a few in hope –
For her mini kingdom to revive.

Whilst flying she becomes tired and buzzes to herself
"That looks like a nice place to land"

And like birds to a hippopotamus that pick out the parasites
In grey tones, though smooth with a shiny surface,
The Queen Bee rests a moment upon Metal-Man's –
Left tool boxed shoulder.

A wee buzz voice sings in his –
Funnel cupped ear, to pour oil
It coils around his ticking cogs
Picking up signals from a small life form.

Metal-man's head turns, clunk, click, clunk, click
To hear the Bees small *"Hello"*

"*Hollo-e*" was Metals-man's reply
With his distant internal electrical hummed voice.

In his diagonal red streaked eye
The look of a saddened warm flame
Dwindling and flickering his last cry.
And with few bleeps he says

"What is your name?"

She quickly buzzed

"Bumbleine, and to this, a moment
To catch the sun, I lean"

She was not scared of him
Could Metal-man understand?
This privileged land.

Bumbleine asks

"What is your name?"

His eager chirped bleep

"Metal Man,
A tin, tin can
To kick and ping
With throwing stones that land
To crack and ting,
Where from a distance –
Every one stands."

Buzz, buzz
Flickering her wings,
Then a quick hover and land
Twice in her anxious dance.

"Why?" she asks in her concerning zippy hum.

Bleep, bleep
A bit of smoke, as a smoker's puffed ring
Billowed from his funnelled ear –
As a long process ticked.

Then he explains his story…

"I was a man back then, Charles Sievad
Working for NASA,
And during a mission into space
As an astronaut, with my suit, floating in dimensions
A void and an illustrated self-contained station
An illusion with some kind of metal to face.

It was during the repair of a spaceship
Called the 'Super-lunar drifter'
From the black of space –
Another piece of metal emerged
What did the crew think?
An alien to face
When suddenly exploding, a ray surged.

Ironically the piece of metal shielded me,
And surrounded by this metal
The ray pushed me into the earth's atmosphere
That fused me together with it
And I was in great fear.

Junk metal left in space clung to me,
And the things that I magnetized on my way down,
Clipping Spoons and silver trays
Tool boxes, oil cans and various tools
Utensils and gizmos
And mechanical machinery,
Which helped to aid my fiery land
With a touch surface cool.
Frosted in white smoke, as if liquid nitrogen
Welded in iron ore.
Sticking to my skin
I was at the core.

I crash landed in a jungle
NASA having lost me –
Covered up the accident with a cloak and dagger.

And now I stagger

To collapse, where I lay
Seized up to a silent halt
An impregnable vault
Birds land on me
Tigers lay asleep on top of my body part
While green grew up around.

My main body is a box
With many little containers and doors
To hold – a secret place
To store

Some screws
Dust 'N' rust, Nuts 'N' Bolts
To tighten when needed,
I have handy tools
Akin to the back of some garage.

Just metal
Round and tinned canned
To bend at the joints
It is time to – rust
The colours are quite impressive.

Old dead spiders
Musty letters
Smelling from unopened dreams
As oil drips dirty
I am patched and soldered at rusty corners.

An inspector gadget finger
I vibrate to music
Echoing in boxed memories
Sounds rebound in a tinned inner world.

No one would open –
  From metal man's boxes
Seeing only to laser a flower.

One day I twitched and moved
Then rapidly a bleep, bleep
My toe seemed to have a spoon –
Projecting from it

"Hollo-e" I said –
To the surrounding inhabitants
The Tiger pelted and jumped off
Because of my unpredicted activity.

The clothed undergrowth moves
To a surge of sound,
The clearing of animals and birds to hide
Now unseen and elusive
Where the only thing heard was a rustle,
And the cracking underfoot
To my treading to silence
That vibrates to flicker my lights,
As my heavy body slowly moved
To a crash and coil, clunk and ring.
Clash clunk ring, clash clunk ring, clash clunk ring...

Big marbled forest drops
As it started to Rain to a hollow tap
"Pit-pat
Rusty spat
Tick-flick
A cheeky wink
Ping-pong
Am I right or wrong?

Sadly and sluggishly
I move with diagonal eyes
In search for my dreams.
And that is my storey.

Bumbleine –
Still perched on his right tool boxed shoulder
Buzzes a song –

"To open a door of Metal-man
Flutters butterfly idea of craft
To try and capture
Butterflies net to chloroform
Knocked out for display
Pinned, in fluffed powered painting.
Each door a different surprise
To whom they once thought
As if hulk,
And this I tell you, Hulk can sulk.

Your metal armoury
Drops as a shield, to lie down
In under tones fluff,
The pigeons pink
Quite a soft blotted paper
As the desert rains to soak."

Confused at Bumbleine's encouragement
He bleeps:

"To what is around
The best you give
For me to oil these old coughing pipes
Hopefully I won't pump out carbon dioxide
Chugging from my metal heart."

Fuzz, buzz, she flusters

"Oh; but this a shield for many enemies
That metal man has
Bad that you might be
You do not flee
To give as a monster can often
In the darkest of places something grows."

Metal man's head in a 360, spins
Whiz zzzzzzzzzip whiz zzzzzzzzzip, whiz, zzzzzzzzzip

Then blurting his response

"What about the angry door
So often opened
Painfully stiff,
Joints are metal sheeting
In my rigid corrugated movement.
If I could loosen these screws?
Then in my outer form –
I could shine, not in the lies of brushed aluminium
But to correspond to an honest inner being
Rather than the dialectics of lies
But rather a white to white."

Metal man clumsily moves to the edge of a nearby lake
He slowly bends down on one knee
And looks at himself in the reflection and continues

"In a mirror, a window
A sight to a parallel universe
The reflection of the upside down mountain
In glistening still waters
That lay deep in Prussian blue.
The birds upside down mate
Hovers close, as a swift to contours' touch
Flies 'ripple effect' of disturbance
Undulate to lapping edge
As tears plop from red rust.
Gathered and deposited
As residue of corrosive salt.

You see, I am a monster
Colourful treads, a streak
By the maker
To hope upon this day,

So Mrs Bumbleine, Buzz and fuzz
Cos' you can't sting me'
Healing properties to induce me

Like oil to run smoother, a lubrication."

Silence as life's questions are hard to answer;
But honey dewed amber in tree sap, runs tears.
Flying to the other shoulder she appears
And says:

"But surely you were made like batman
This to whom
Goodness you may sway
As dancers to combine
To make something fine

Why cry then 'Metal Man'?
Metal with oiled sheeting
Valves, pumps and hydraulic workings –
Cannot run salt tears to rust.
Your anger will subdue
If to love and to be present
Then to remove.

Do not dwell,
Dwell is a means of end
Surely, it is by two, a friend
To bring out of mirrors elusions
That lures from trying,
Or to make an amends.

Oh I look beyond what I see, it is not an electric light;
But a glint in your eye, not of a white glare, nor blue
Rather an inner reflection of your human spirit
I look through, look through and have hope in you.

Metal-man turns his head and looks at the Queen Bee
With his flickering eye and says

"O, Bumbleine
What shall I do?"

Excited she promptly opened one of his doors –
On his big squared body and said

"Well, Charles,
As a small fish to a whale
I will live with you
A door I can retreat
Beside your written mail."

Metal man proudly states:

"I would not let you fluster in these letters
To go stale
You can come and go as you please
And leave your honey scented trail
For your friends –
Your whereabouts you telltale."

Metal man moves as slow as a snail
So off they went, friends
His thudding feet
With her whispered buzz of amber love.

Together in a world with dark enemies
To try and bring justice
Without prejudice.

Pink

Giro Italia, 9th April 2014

Paint the town pink
Clint Eastwood would be impressed;
But it was the pale pink
Rider – spraying bikes pink
Racing a currant through,
Like surges of wind
A gush,
As if cycling past –
Covering the town pink
For grey tried to speak
Hush, hush now –
Sprayed and covered in pink ink.

What string connected the cyclists?
Trust from a hidden link.

I woke up,
Twice I had to blink
Yesterday surely the town was of a normal
Middle ranged tone,
And all that I could think, was pink.

Taffy's Daffodils

(The Daffodil trilogy, poem 2)

If you and I would wear a leek in our hair
Then I would know we were friends
Because, I would be close enough to see it
The land is too small to separate from.

I hold sight of pictures and memories
As if the landscapes voice is in my heart,
To hear their giggles,
Like the gurgles of a river over stones.

A corolla nimbus of circulating six petals,
Each yoked in birth
In the middle spewing fourth a trumpet.
Oh these crispate edges, living near.

I Hold the petal between my finger and thumb
To press, squeeze and rub
It produces a natural watercolour ink
Just to leave a yellow streak on a page.

Its translucent behaviour,
The sun, this shine of cadmium sulphide,
Glitters in blackness
My fingers shadow behind tracing paper.

In quiet fleeing,
My finger and thumb go up to my eyes
As if holding back two dams,
My tear stung fingers are rubbed into my hand.

I lean forward to inhale a sweet linger of fragrance
Particles of pollen, yellow talcum-powder
It fills my head and lungs,
So that I can resonate my voice to call Louder.

Taffodils

(The Daffodil Trilogy, poem 3)

Shush, you're bright yellow –
Is speaking to loudly in this silence
Reminding me…
Eyes to see and look upon
Trumpeting to my vision,
Its bloomed instrument to play.

Hold this sight of us
A bunch, a few
Holding in view
Laid loosely in a vase.
I have a crush with such beauty;
But I am afraid of my crush,
From my hand that can hold a petal –
Of such colour as with you.

This manner of such impromptu
Can only exist when you are not aware,
Like these daffodils –
That are blind to their own beauty
These yellow blossoms –
That shine upon my grey face

Like Buttercups –
And their sun golden reflection
Held under my chin, to say that –
"I like butter"

My Eastern Promise

You are like the origin of tea
Always in the flavour and colour

It could have been a tease
Like a rare bird showing himself,
The fluttered colour is at a glance
I just recognised its plumage –
        In its moment of ease

To write its name on a bird spotting list
It belonged in the garden,
A song-bird so easy to please.

Oh Lacquer work –
On the black bird, which is Chinese
Oil shinned in subtle satin,
The fanned tail had a breeze
As if it was spread,
Displayed on the wall of your house
Like a princess of the ancient dynasties.

The black bird sings his fluted song
In the cherry trees
This Chinese vision of blossom
Welcoming –
        The garden with summer greeneries.

Oh, cleave to the elegant oriental shape
That joins the head and the tail
A saddle between two mountains

Pyrography beak of a vivid bright orange
As if setting afloat in the light –
            Of a Chinese lantern,
Or flying like a dart upon the wing.

Trail

(Silver-lining)

Autumn's leaves
Lying so beautifully on the ground
Drizzled in fine rain,
Though areas still relatively crispy
The wind could quite easily shift them
As I looked and studied its twinkle
These little details
Of star coated leaves.

Similar to the shiny silky trail –
Of a snail
To his whereabouts, a written mail
A single track
Leading to the undergrowth
To eat luscious leaves

In a summer evening
When it is warm and humid –
Follow his shiny silky mail
Of Bodily mucus to secrete
A hovercraft on slime
To glide over the rough concrete.

Being vertical or upside down –
It acts as glue
Its insides are displayed –
With its seemingly ugly form
Of soft tissue.

This is a gastropod
A moving stomach
Of a slow onward plod
An action of discharge
Writing in the quality of silk,
It's what it leaves, to see

Never to flee

Stretched and hooked –
Over protruding substratum
Like a distant silvery stream
Reflecting with the light.

Perhaps the Milky Way
Long clouds of twinkling clusters
Looped and laced as an aesthete,

To catch sight of his trail
It is as if, frost looked upon concrete –
Glistening in the moonlight?

In the open –
Of a large space
His pace is not safe
Quiet and discreet
When suddenly walked on!
'Crack'
A quake, like a cornflake.
Crisp in its freshness,
A crunch so frail.

It has left a small legacy
In this wonder land of a garden,
Leads to a Song Thrushes dish
Black Birds wait for scrap
From the shells wrap.

Shake the little blue packages of death
Slug pellets churn and melt
Burn through, to dry
So that it may die
Foaming and curling like a worm
Bubbling with puss
As if from the mouth
Or drooled in sedation.

This percentage
In an all edible leaved passage,

Where is protection in the night?
Where; but from harm?
It whirls, and leaves his mail.

On leaves that twinkle
Showing where they have been.

Rejection

Feeding in over exuberance
From the trees leaves,
Little Aphides in slew
Sucking more than they need
It is the sight of rue
Upon your summer countenance,
Deep dewy-eyed in satin glare
A swelling from the tear gland
It builds up in the Aphides
To ooze its sweet goo
Then in excess in the canopies –
It begins to rain honey dew,
It is but messy and untidy
As it drips through…
Leaving patches, spots and splats
With a course of action to pursue.

Prejudice against Coffee Drinkers

In tribute and response to David Braziel
(Created with the help from the Hosford group.)

Would you like to go for coffee?
As if everybody is a coffee drinker
Even the place is called a café,
Abbreviated as to be French, the bourgeois
You cannot even say
"Do you want to go for a cup of tea?"
Without offending the coffee drinkers.

This political correctness with the words –
'Hot beverage'
Chi-tea latte they just sit on the fence
Can tea and coffee people ever agree?

Have you heard the sound of coffee being made?
Bang, bang tssshhh, tssshhh; bang, bang, bang
I am trying to read in this café, you know!

Or putting on the coffee machine at home,
Waiting for the Filter – Drip, drip, drip; drip, drip, drip
It just builds up the bladder,
And dried processed coffee
It's just not good enough
It is all a bit diuretic for me
As the Coffee drinkers are always running to the toilet.

They complain at the tea drinkers –
Having too much of a variety;
When these coffee drinkers
Have their, espressos, double espressos
Latte, Americano, cappachina and mocha
That's not including all the flavours of
Carmel, orange, mint and vanilla, and etc.

I wonder…

Is it to hide the bitter taste of coffee?
Really they are secret tea drinkers –
Who like to sit in quiet spaces
To nit-natter, or to be thinkers.

It's just not my latte;
But I can't say that
I am not a coffee drinker
It's just not my cup of tea
English breakfast, earl grey
And mint could be for me.

Tea cosies and mittens
From the snow
"The kettles on!"
How about a tea house
Old people want to relax
Made as quiet as a mouse.

Anyone care for a chocolate?
Passing around the box only to be left –
            With the coffee fondant flavour
"No, on second thoughts –
I'll give the chocolate a miss."

These coffee drinkers
They never slow down
Always fidgety and twitchy
Always a hard worked frown

Coffee is a night to stay up
Work, work, work
Fetch me a cup of coffee
I am tired
No fuss
Here is another cup of coffee
Or pro-plus
Just keep it a lit
You are a professional business man

In need to get that extra stimulant hit

Well, I am going to get a quiet cup of tea
You won't find me at the local power station
Creating energy.

Happy Endings

From a spot of rain
Comes rust
An orange, peeling like a tangerine
Flacking, or dust like spores
As a fungi to blow in the wind
Millions, to shake the coat
And there, is star dust

Not like a romantic film
Tries for this containment
Never in winter days
What I mean,
If happiness has to end, then…
Here after
Winter descends –
            To
This end is not contained
Not to be;
But as a lover and friend.

It's like the Hazel tree
These dust pollens
Catkins dangle yellow
Or capsules and suspended subtle of orange
Blows, settles and catches
Maybe latch
Hatch in soft hazel brown.

Not like a romantic film
Tries for this containment
Never in winter days
What I mean,
If happiness has to end, then…
Here after
Winter descends –
            To

This end is not contained
Not to be;
But as a lover and friend.

Here after
The nakedness, the shedding
The destitute,
    Cold winds and frost bite
Long this black night
It holds this vow
It is written in the ground
Written in brown
The first sight of snow drops
In quiet places
    In small colour.

Thank you –
To my mum for her input in my work and encouragement, and for just being Mum
Thank you –
To Tracy Chan, my (Princess Chanettia) for her reassurance, praise and encouragement, and for her help with the designs and illustrations. I am her number one fan xx (- ;
Thank you –
To my Auntie Joan for helping me with corrections on a few of the poems, and her support.
Thank you –
To Arlene and Mary for their support and encouragement.
Thank you –
To the central library librarians for their support, input and encouragement, particularly Nicky and Karen
Thank you –
To Jim Mclean for support and encouragement
Thank you –
To the charity 'Inspire' particularly Deirdre (Dee)
For Mixed jam, her support and encouragement.

Even though he is hiding, I thank God who created the heavens, the earth and the oceans and everything in them and upon them.

Thank you to all the bands, singers and musicians that I admire, there are too many to list. They have been an inspiration to my writing, and somewhere to run to in all this madness.

Past thank you

Thank you to my art teacher from Orangefield high school, without him I would have left with no GCSEs; but because he cared, I left with a 'C' grade in GCSE art and design giving me that little bit of confidence.

I thank all my art teachers in Castlereagh College, Ray Duncan, Ian Fleming and Wills
And my tutors through university (Hull school of Art & Design) for pushing me in the direction of poetry and philosophy.

87720187R00100

Made in the USA
Columbia, SC
26 January 2018